Lost Souls: FOUND!

Inspiring Sto...

Kyla Duffy and Lowrey Mumford

Published by Happy Tails Books™, LLC

Happy Tails Books™ uses the power of storytelling to affect positive change in the lives of animals in need. The joy, hope, and (occasional) chaos these stories describe will make you laugh and cry as you em*bark* on a journey with these authors, who are guardians and/or fosters of rescued dogs. "Reading for Rescue" with Happy Tails Books not only brings further awareness to animal advocacy efforts and breed characteristics, but each sale also results in a financial contribution to dog rescue efforts.

Lost Souls: Found!™ Inspiring Stories About Dogs by Kyla Duffy and Lowrey Mumford

Published by Happy Tails Books™, LLC www.happytailsbooks.com

The publisher gratefully acknowledges the numerous dog rescue groups and their members, who generously granted permission to use their stories and photos.

The following brand names are registered trademarks and the property of their owners. The author and publishing company make no claims to the logos mentioned in this book including: Petfinder.com, Petsmart, PETCO, Walmart, Citibank, Vaseline, Skype, Dingo

Photo Credits (All Rights Reserved by Photographers):

Front Cover: *Bella*, Kelly Dunn, www.justimagineinc.com
Back Cover Top: *Dakota*, Kelly Dunn
Back Cover L: *Eli*, Kelly Dunn
Back Cover Mid: *Maggie and Mulligan*, Kelly Dunn
Back Cover R: *Daisy*, Ashley Johnson, www.lovemuttphotography.com

Publishers Cataloging In Publication

Lost Souls: Found!™ Inspiring Stories About Dogs/ [Compiled and edited by] Kyla Duffy and Lowrey Mumford.

p. ; cm.

ISBN: 978-0-9826964-5-3

1. Dogs. 2. Dog rescue. 3. Dogs – Anecdotes. 4. Animal welfare – United States. 5. Human-animal relationships – Anecdotes. I. Duffy, Kyla. II. Mumford, Lowrey. III. Title.

SF426.5   2011

636.7   2010915177

Rescue Resources:

Confessions From the Shelter:
What you didn't want to know
http://confessionsfromtheanimalshelter.com

Dog Breed Info Center:
Learn about breed characteristics
http://www.dogbreedinfo.com

Mill Dog Manifesto:
Free eBook about puppy mills
http://happytailsbooks.com/milldog

Petfinder.com:
Find an adoptable pet
http://petfinder.com

Pit Bull Resource Central:
Pit Bull advocacy information
http://pbrc.net

*Want more information about the dogs, authors, and rescues
featured in this book? http://happytailsbooks.com*

Table of Contents

Introduction: Scouting Talent

We have been writing the *Lost Souls: Found!* series for just over a year now, and through the various breed-specific editions, we've highlighted the special moments rescued dogs and their humans have shared that have truly touched both lives.

If you've ever found, rescued, or adopted a dog *and given them a chance to adjust and blossom*, you've surely felt their deep understanding of the gift you've given them. And you know that adopted dogs are *not* just the rejects, the bottom-feeders, and the losers. Purebred or mixed-breed, these dogs are generally wonderful animals who possess the capacity to love and be loved, just like dogs who were acquired as puppies from reputable breeders. The only difference is that these dogs were born into unfortunate circumstances and sometimes require patience and encouragement to help them move beyond their previous traumas.

The director of *Indecent Proposal*, Adrian Lyne, knew there was something special about adoptable dogs, as he specifically requested one to be in the film. Here's the story as told by Hollywood studio wrangler Kathryn Segura:

Two decades ago I was working on the film Indecent Proposal starring Robert Redford, Woody Harrison, and Demi Moore. The director, Adrian Lyne, wanted to put a dog in the film, so he hired me as the animal wrangler/coordinator for the film. I called the animal rental companies in town for an open audition, and after two days of looking at dogs, Adrian asked me to go to a shelter and rescue a dog. He thought the others were fine, but that just didn't have "it."

The next day I went to the Burbank Animal Shelter. I found a great dog and took his picture to show Adrian. He loved the look of the dog and gave his approval. But when I went back to the shelter, they told me it was a first come, first serve with adoptions, meaning one had to come to the shelter in the middle of the night and wait until the doors opened if they wanted a particular dog. They said if I arrived by 2 a.m., I should be able to get the dog I wanted, so I did exactly that.

By 2 a.m. on the nose, I was the second car in the parking lot! I waited all night until the guard came out at 7 a.m. to let us in. And yes, you guessed it; the other car was also there for the same dog.

They adopted the dog, and as I was leaving with my head hung low, one of the animal control people came running up to me. She told me that someone had turned in a five-month-old Lab mix that I should take a look at. I followed her back to see this dog. When I went up to her run, she peed all over herself. We took her out, so I could spend some time with her. Since she was an owner surrender, she could be adopted straight away.

I knew that no matter what, she was going to be my dog. I named her Chloe', and she became the dog in the film. She had her own trailer on set, and I trained her as Adrian directed me about what she needed to do. The LA Times found out about Chloe' and did a story about her. She was the greatest dog ever. She went from pound puppy to movie star!

Some might say that if rescue dogs are good enough for Hollywood, they're good enough for us all, as Hollywood often sets the bar for what many aspire to be. Let's ALL aspire to be rescuers!

We created this volume of *Lost Souls: Found!* to show the rainbow of colorful, dazzling, unique dogs available for adoption. We've included mixed-breeds and purebreds to demonstrate this diversity. But despite the differences between the breeds, one thing is consistent: The authors of these stories share a unique bond with their pets, who have irreversibly enriched their lives.

We hope this book will inspire you to to check out a shelter or rescue the next time you are ready for the furry adventure of a lifetime. It's not always easy, but adoption is undeniably an adventure you don't want to miss!

 *Kyla Duffy & Lowrey Mumford*

Inspiring Stories About Dogs

"We can judge the heart of a man by his treatment of animals."

- Immanuel Kant

Charlie Takes a Dip

Charlie and I live in New York City and like to visit Central Park in the morning during off-leash hours. While Charlie never strays too far from me, he loves running around free in the grass. On this particular morning, we were walking along the bank of a pretty large pond in the middle of the park. Charlie ventured to the edge of the pond, but since he had never shown any interest in water before, I let him wander. Then, he started to cautiously step in to the dirty, muddy, and moldy pond.

At this point I was amused but still not too worried. That's when Charlie started to actually swim in the pond! He headed straight to the middle of the dark and disgusting water, and I feared he might get tired, stop swimming, and then have no way to get back to land. I called to him, I whistled for him, and I looked around for someone to help me, but in the wee hours of morning, even in New York, people were few and far between.

Charlie, normally a very obedient dog, was completely ignoring my panicked cries. He looked so calm and happy that someone watching him would surely have thought he was just going for his morning swim. My nervousness was growing quickly, and I realized that my best option was to jump into the murky water after him and try to catch up. My heart was racing as I started thinking of the possibilities of this dire situation. I took off my jacket. I was planning on taking off my t-shirt, too, so that I'd have something clean and dry to wear when I got out, when I heard a jogger from the other side of the pond: "Stop! Wait, don't jump in!"

I screamed, "But that's my dog, and he's not coming back to me!"

The jogger replied, "He's coming toward me. Just wait, and I'll catch him!"

I thought, okay, we can try this option before I jump in.

Charlie did continue swimming to the other end of the pond, looking as happy as a clam. Then, when Charlie was about five feet away from the shore, he turned around back towards the middle of the pond! I was beside myself, but I realized that Charlie was clearly teasing us and enjoying every bit of it. Eventually Charlie came back to my side of the shore and trampled out of the water. Everything but his head was a muddy, greenish-brown mess! I felt a rush of emotions: relief, happiness, and anger. And I couldn't stop laughing as I tried to dry Charlie off with my jacket.

 *The Sheth Family*

Need a Lift

I don't remember what day of the week it was or even the season, but it's still a day that will remain in my memory forever. As I drove into the small town of Arcadia, Wisconsin, my intention was to find a coffee table for my living room. I had no idea that I would be bringing home something more essential to a home than a piece of furniture.

As I drove past a gas station, I noticed something on the side of the road. Had I not been traveling with my three dogs,

I may have passed it by, thinking it was an old piece of carpet. But the dogs started to raise a ruckus in the backseat, so I turned around in the parking lot and drove by for a second look. To my utter dismay, a very dirty, almost unrecognizable dog was sitting there on the side of a busy thoroughfare!

I pulled over and jumped out of the car, afraid the poor fellow was about to get hit by the traffic whizzing past. The sounds of my dogs barking in the car seemed to hold his interest until I could kneel down beside him. Being a professional dog groomer, I had seen dirty and matted dogs come into my shop, but nothing prepared me for this. He leaned warily against me as I talked soothingly to him, all the while running my fingers over his filthy coat looking for some sort of identification. I found nothing except a pine cone matted to his rear leg, a wad of gum stuck between his toes, ears encrusted with black goop, and burrs everywhere. One quick look told me he was a male and he wasn't neutered.

I had no idea how long he had been running or how long it had been since his last meal. I carefully picked him up and was amazed at how light he was under all of the excess hair. I placed him on a towel my back seat, where he was happily greeted by my wiggling threesome. He sat, looking dazed and exhausted. After a trip to area businesses and some unfamiliar neighborhoods, I decided the best thing to do was to get him some food and water and continue my search over the phone. I looked in the back seat, and he was curled in a tight ball, sleeping as best he could on the bumpy ride home.

Back at my grooming shop, I got to work trying to find the dog within all the matted hair and debris this boy had inadvertently collected on his travels. He stood on the grooming table as I slowly started to unveil what turned out to be a very handsome, white-and-buff, parti-colored Cocker Spaniel. He let me wash his ears and trim his nails. I talked to him as he stared out the window, and I decided to call him Freeway.

Days went by and no one answered any of the ads I had placed in local papers. No one responded to the posters I put up in Arcadia. This dog seemed to have appeared out of thin air. I took him to my vet, who determined that Freeway had a bad case of ear mites—most likely from bunking with farm cats. Aside from that, Freeway was fit as a fiddle, and the vet thought him to be about two years old. I made an appointment to have him neutered the next day.

Freeway fit into my canine family as well as if I had gotten him as a pup; it was as if my dogs sensed he needed a family in the worst way, and they became very close to him. But alas, four dogs in any house is a lot of dogs, and I decided to see if any of my clients were interested in taking in my little stray.

It didn't take long before one of my regular clients took a shine to this charming little man. Freeway went to live with some wonderful people and their Airedale named Liberty. The two of them became inseparable. I got to see Freeway every three weeks for a trim and a bath, and every time I picked him up at his new home, he sat proudly in the front seat of my van, while the other dogs rode in kennels in the back. He always had "Freezie love" for me—this was when he would stand on his hind legs and put a paw on either of my shoulders to give me a hug while I was kneeling. He lived a happy, carefree life with his new family, and they loved him immensely, never forgetting to tell me how lucky they were that Freeway had ended up with them. I couldn't agree with them more. If ever a dog needed a family, it was little Freeway.

Sadly, Freeway developed cancer at age 12, and after doing all that they could to help him, the family was left with no other choice than to put him out of his pain. I received a tearful phone call from Freeway's family the day he died, thanking me again for picking up the little dog on the side of the road. As I hung up the phone and cried for the matted dog who so badly needed a family, I also shed tears of joy that he had found one that loved him as much as they had for so many years.

 *Amy Conway*

Where did My Puppy Go?

Wrinkles was found in a large pineapple field on the west side of Maui when he was a couple weeks old. He arrived at the humane society just before my husband and I went for a visit. As soon as I saw this little puppy, with a wrinkly face like an an old man, I fell in love. Wrinkles had a large head attached to a little body. His shiny black coat, caramel eyes, and black marks on his tongue made us wonder what kind of breeds he came from.

We couldn't resist and brought the little guy home with us. Wrinkles adapted to us and fit in with our routine quickly. He was surprisingly easy to care for and housetrained within a week. We were thrilled to have a dog in our lives again, making us a family of three.

One afternoon we were preoccupied with my broken-down car and didn't notice that Wrinkles was missing until it was almost dark. At first we didn't believe our dog had run away, but after searching for him everywhere around our home, we knew he was gone. We drove my husband's truck around the neighborhood looking for Wrinkles until exhaustion finally forced us to retire for the night.

The next day I was up with the sun. While readying myself to start searching again, I heard a noise outside. I walked through our back yard and noticed something moving inside my broken car. When I opened the back door, Wrinkles hopped out looking happy and rested!

He is five years old now, a gentle Black Lab/Shar Pei mix with the face of an old man and the sparkling eyes of a puppy. Wrinkles is a unique blend of kindness and companionship that wakes us every day with a smile (us) and a lick (him), and he no longer sleeps in the car.

 *Celia Lumsden*

The Flower Girl

When my husband and I first decided to add a four-legged child to our family, we purchased a Golden Retriever from a local breeder. We had 12 wonderful years with Casey before we lost him to a stroke. Although we were heartbroken, we started thinking about adopting our next "kids" from a rescue organization.

As we read stories of rescued Golden Retrievers, we knew that our mission was not only to rescue a couple of these orphaned dogs but to rescue older or special needs dogs. When we arrived at the local pet supply store where rescue organizations have "meet and greet" days, we walked down the aisle and immediately saw the most beautiful face looking in our direction. There, lying on the cool floor, was a strawberry blonde girl with beautiful, big eyes. We were smitten. Thinking that she probably was there with her family, because a gorgeous girl like that would surely have a home, we stopped to tell her how pretty she was. That's when we found out that she was available for adoption.

As we knelt to talk to Molly, we were told by her foster mom that she was approximately seven years old. She had been a stray at one time, but she had lived with a family for the previous year. Molly had been lying in their driveway one day when she was accidentally run over. Her hip was crushed, so her owners took her to the vet, but they could not afford to pay for the surgery. Molly was left with the vet and once again became an orphan. The vet contacted Tennessee Valley Golden Retriever Rescue (TVGRR), and thus began Molly's next stage of life. TVGRR put her in a foster home, where she was evaluated for any further health problems. Along with the crushed hip, Molly was heartworm positive, had allergies, and had a large mass on her side. After successfully undergoing treatment for heartworm, Molly was scheduled to have her hip repaired and was ready for adoption.

We took Molly for a walk through the store, and as we talked to her and petted her long, silky fur, we immediately fell in love. Everything about Molly was big. She was tall with huge eyes, big feet, long toes, and a tail that would drag the ground when she was standing. There was no doubt Molly was the "daughter" we wanted to add to our family, so we adopted this beautiful girl and her new "brother," Trooper, on a sunny day in July.

We had a week to get to know our new kids before Molly had her hip surgery. When we picked up our big girl after her surgery, she looked like a patchwork quilt because she had large patches of fur removed for the hip repair, the mass removal on her opposite side, and the application of a pain patch on her back. Of course, with time the hair grew back, and the long silken locks again became beautiful.

After Molly's hip improved, we learned that she was a typical Golden Retriever ball-chaser. She tired easily, but she loved to chase a tennis ball and always had a ball near for chewing and chasing. We thought the tennis ball would be Molly's favorite means of entertainment, until one summer day when we discovered her true passion. It was a dry summer in Knoxville, Tennessee, and the flowers required regular watering in order to survive the lack of rain. As I uncoiled the water hose, Molly walked away, and my thought was that she was wary of the hose, as is the case with some dogs.

As I began watering the thirsty flowers, Molly turned, charged across the yard, and snapped at the nozzle, spraying water all over herself and *her mom*. To my amazement, she continued to bite at the water as it spewed from the nozzle and sprayed in every direction. There was little water hitting the flowers; most of it was entertaining Molly. This began a new favorite game: helping mom water the flowers. From here on out, it would take at least twice as long to do the watering, with Molly's help. There were times when she would lie down, being so tired from all the "helping," and it would seem that she would not be able to run again. But it didn't take long for the water to call to Molly, and if there was one ounce of strength left in those long legs, her weak hips would push her up and propel her toward the water.

When the watering was complete and the hose was once again coiled on its stand, our beautiful girl was always temporarily replaced by a soaking wet urchin, who appeared to have dreadlocks on her head. Although water dripped from head to tail, we were happy to see her playing this wonderful new game.

Since Molly helped with watering the flowers, she must have decided that it would be good to help pick the flowers as well. As she walked by a clump of just-opened day lilies, she chomped off a flower and then went skipping across the yard with it in her mouth, a bounce in her step, and a smile on her face. She allowed several flowers to bloom in full glory, but just when we thought she had forgotten about the tasty flowers, she would casually walk by the latest blooms, bite the freshest one, and once again, go skipping across the yard. Our flowers suffered during the reign of Molly, the flower girl, but it was hard to get too mad at her because she seemed so happy when she was out "picking" flowers.

Our big girl continued to help her mom with the flowers for four wonderful years. We lost Molly to cancer after that time, making this summer much quieter and sadder than the previous four summers. Watering the flowers is finished quickly, and all the flower blooms remain until they simply fade away. The flower gardens look pretty, but we long for the days when the watering took twice as long and the blooms were always at risk of being eaten by a beautiful, big, silky-haired girl named Molly.

Our time was too short with Molly, but we were able to experience the joy of this big-hearted, loving girl, and she knew that she had a family who cared for her, loved her passionately, and happily let her play the most wonderful game in the world of helping her mom take care of the flowers.

 *Elizabeth A. Whited*

A Wildfire Blessing

Because of the fires in the area of my imprisonment—I can't call it a home because my whole life was in a cage—the leg people, whom I only ever saw from the knees down, had to evacuate. It started with the strong smell of smoke and a lot of noise from the leg people frantically throwing stuff in their car and then peeling out of the driveway. Then there was silence. The only sound I heard was from other prisoners in cages like mine. They were crying. We were trapped, and there was nothing we could do. I just drifted in and out of sleep until I heard a lot of noise from some humans—different ones from the usual leg people. These humans picked me and my fellow prisoners up and took us to a doggy doctor.

We were all in bad shape. The humans who sprung us from our imprisonment didn't think they could save us, but they called Dachshund Adoption, Rescue, and Education (DARE) to help us. DARE took nine of us into their care, including me, a Doxie/Xolo mix. I may not be a pure Doxie, but I am a Doxie-wannabe, or what you would call a naked Doxie—I don't have any fur. I was part of a breeding experiment gone horribly wrong.

With these new people, for the first time in my life I felt the gentle caress of a human hand. I felt the warmth of a human hug and heard the sound of a caring human voice. This was amazing to me, as I didn't understand human love. Back in that prison, every time a human approached me, I would tremble in fear. It seemed that whenever humans came near, they hurt me. Sometimes dirty hands would shove some food and slimy water into my cage or take away my babies, but that was the only human contact I ever had. I just spent the first part of my life making puppies, over and over. I never felt the warm sunshine on my back or grass under my paws. You can understand why I was surprised at meeting *nice* people.

A DARE foster mommy took me home to nurse my wounds and heal my heart. She showed me not to fear humans and how to feel love. The other foster doggies showed me how to play with them and with toys. Up until then, I had never even seen a toy!

When my foster mommy decided I was ready for a forever home, she took me and other foster Doxies to an adoption event. There I met a really nice human who carried me around all day. She was worried that I might get sunburned, so she put some nice lotion on me, so I wouldn't burn. I really felt loved when she held me in her arms that day. I wanted her to take me home, but she wasn't ready yet because she was new to the foster program and still learning how to be a foster mommy.

Another foster Doxie and I were placed in a forever home; at least we thought it was going to be forever, but it didn't work out. After two months, we learned that DARE was going to come and get us. Later that night, a miracle happened. That really nice human with the soothing lotion came and scooped me up in her arms and took me home with her. This was to be my real forever home, and I couldn't have been happier!

Whenever I smell smoke, it takes me back to how awful my life was before those wildfires. But for me, smoke is a happy smell. It's the scent of freedom, and the symbol of a new beginning.

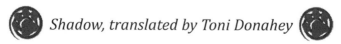 *Shadow, translated by Toni Donahey*

With Love and Luck

"With a little love and luck, you will get by." -Jimmy Buffet

"**N**o promises. We are just looking today," David said as we drove to the adoption event. Funny he should say that because David was the one who wanted a puppy. But I was the one who knew she was my dog in less than five minutes. When she sat in my lap, looked up, and flicked her long, wet, pink tongue under my chin, I knew. I stroked her soft puppy-fur and felt the long strands between my fingers. I fiddled with the tiny blue collar that looked like it could be a newborn's bracelet: It said she was puppy number 777.

"She's lucky!" I exclaimed, her puppy breath spreading over my fingers, which she mindlessly gnawed. Tears welled up in my eyes as I felt the inexplicable joy of finding my new companion. David, who saw how happy I was, agreed to adopt her, and we proceeded to wander around the store hosting the adoption event like new parents, imagining what our new addition would need.

We drove home, with the puppy's warm body curled up in a little ball on my lap. I thought nothing in my life could go wrong with the world's cutest and sweetest puppy warming my legs and a wonderful and loving boyfriend by my side. We named her Layla (my choice). David told people it was after the Eric Clapton song, but I loved the story: an ancient Arabic poem about being driven mad by the love of Layla, a princess and "beauty of the night." That's how I felt—this puppy became my life as I became more and more enamored with her beauty.

Layla was rescued from Raton, New Mexico. She was the runt of the litter at about seven pounds. A beautiful Lab/ Border Collie mix, her litter was found on the side of the road in a duffel bag. Everyone who meets Layla asks, "Who could do such a thing?" It's something I, too, wonder and will never understand.

Months later David proposed, and I was elated to grow our own little family. The three of us settled in to a happy routine. David and I spent days walking Layla to the dog park just to let her play. We took her when we went skiing in Vail at Christmas. We had to ring the bottom of the Christmas tree with bells because Layla was a chewer, and we were worried about her eating the tree or ornaments. She would hit the bells on the tree, so we could hear when she got too close. David had a remote control car Layla chased around the house; I remember one time when Layla was chasing the car, and she ran into a table that was covered in wedding magazines. They fell all over and around her, freaking her out. It was so cute...

Everything seemed perfect. But then David changed his mind. He decided he didn't love me. He didn't want to marry me. He broke our engagement, and in the ensuing "splitting up of possessions," David got the house, and I got Layla. I suspect he didn't want responsibility, and that was how he viewed us both. I felt like my life was over, like I was falling apart. At first, I had nowhere to stay, and thus couldn't take Layla with me, so she stayed with David. My body and heart hurt; I felt alone and had no reason to get out of bed.

A friend offered to let Layla and me stay at her house, and I was overjoyed to have my companion back. Layla offered me something that no one else could—a reason to get out of bed in the morning. I had to get up, if only to take Layla out and get her some food. Having Layla forced me to be outside, to walk and exercise, and to get fresh air. I changed the rules of the house, allowing her to cuddle with me on the bed. I loved the feeling of her warm, soft body against me. I cried into her fur: first, every day; then, every other day; then, every couple of days; until I was just crying every once in a while. She was there every step of the way.

Slowly, with Layla's help, I started living again. Layla and I moved into our own apartment. Layla loved running up and down the new stairs, and found a new fun game of dropping her toys off the loft, seemingly aiming at my head. She and

I started going to the dog park again, where we both made new friends. We started running together and hiking in the beautiful open space around Colorado. We climbed our first 14,000-foot mountain (Layla was ready to do another, but after one *I* had had enough) and explored breweries. I've realized Layla is the love of my life (at least right now), and she saved me. I wonder, what would I have done without a reason for getting up—a reason for eating, sleeping, and being?

Layla is my best friend. I consider her my own lucky puppy. Perhaps I saved her life by rescuing her, although I doubt that such a cute and sweet dog wouldn't have been rescued quickly. In the end, I know that she saved my life and continues to be my reason. I know that I have to be okay because no one in the world would love that dog as much as I do. When I adopted Layla, I thought the 777 would mean luck for her. Now I know that all the luck was mine.

 *Jessica Morris*

Light of a New Beginning

Into each life a little rain must fall, which is what happened the day I lost my beloved dog Peanut. Each hour that passed without her seemed like a week. Before she died, I had been looking on Petfinder.com for another dog who might be as "perfect" as my Peanut, and I saw Wendy's photo, but it wasn't until after Peanut passed away during a cancer operation that I became determined to make the long-haired Chihuahua/Beagle mix my own.

I know from volunteering with various animal rescues that adopting an animal from a rescue group usually takes anywhere from a few weeks to a few months, so I set out to try and adopt this perfect little girl with the expectation that it would take a while. To find out more, I got in touch with the foster parent for the Floyd County Humane Society in Virginia, who was responsible for Wendy. She told me that Wendy was affectionate and loved to be held. The downside was that she loved to sleep in a people bed...as long as no one else slept in it with her. Okay—I could get her a dog bed and learn to sleep without my living stuffed animal.

Sunny, Wendy's foster mom, told me to fill out the application and apply for her. She advised me that there were about ten other applications in on Wendy. My thoughts alternated between hoping the sweet little girl went to the right home and, "Please, please, please, pick me!" I dozed off that night thinking about how much I wished I still had my baby Peanut, and how since she wasn't coming back, I wanted Wendy. I think I fell asleep around 2 a.m. and woke up at 6 a.m. feeling like it had been two years since I had held Peanut. I then realized that it had been less than 24 hours. I began my day hoping that I had a reason to head to Virginia to meet my new best friend.

At 7:30 that morning, Sunny called. She told me she had received my application and was going to check my references. I asked when she would let me know the outcome, and she said she would get back to me by 3:30 p.m. I considered taking a very large sleeping pill to pass the time, but instead I just tried to take my mind off Wendy and go about my day.

At 8:45 a.m., the phone rang. It was Sunny, and Wendy was *mine*!

After I hung up, I arranged for a rental car and a hotel room. I then realized it was only Tuesday, and I still had to finish out the work week before driving from Pennsylvania to Virginia. After three long days, my husband and I left at 6:30 on Saturday morning to go meet Wendy. We stopped to watch a Virginia Tech/Miami baseball game for an hour. After all, my husband should get something out of this trip, right? When the game was over, we left for Sunny's house. And when we pulled up in the driveway, there sat my pretty Wendy Endy.

After meeting Wendy, we went to our hotel, and I got my first eight consecutive hours of sleep since Peanut had passed. I woke up ready to pick up my dog and take a five-hour drive home. Wendy sat in the back seat looking out the window most of the way. She kept looking at me like, "Where am I going? And who are you?"

We arrived home and Wendy was greeted by two canine brothers and a sister. A few sniffs here and there and Wendy fit in perfectly. The four of them immediately began playing as if Wendy had been here all along.

Wendy and I have reached an agreement about our sleeping arrangements. She comes up to bed and lies down with me, and after I fall asleep, she gets up and roams the house to find where she wants to sleep. In some ways she acts like my Peanut, and in other ways she is Wendy, a very different dog.

I am grateful to Floyd County Humane Society for speeding up my application and allowing me to adopt Wendy at all, since I was from out of state. Sometimes the process can be much more difficult, but Sunny and the other volunteers made it easy and enjoyable. I cannot say enough nice things about them, and I hope all the other applicants who were interested in Wendy found other dogs in need of rescue.

I heard once that it's impossible to help every dog, but to any dog you can help, you are the world. That may be true, but in our case *Wendy* is *my* world! She has been the bright light at the end of the tunnel that was Peanut's passing, truly helping me to get through it in a way only a dog who has known hardship could.

 *Sandi Endy*

Doggie Doings

Do-Go-What? Angel is our adopted Dogo Argentino, a large, white, muscular breed originally from Argentina. She fit in right away and had no problems adjusting as a member of our family. Because Angel is a unique breed, we are asked many questions about her like, "She's a what?" Occasionally people fear her because of her size, but most are just impressed by her patience and calm nature. I'm about 90 pounds soaking wet, and Angel is large and strong, but she respects my authority and listens to my boys. We couldn't ask for a better family addition! -*Andrea North*

A Fourth-ever Home: A while ago I read an article about the unforeseen impact that the economy was having on animals. People were leaving them in homes or gardens or tied up outside local humane societies because they could no longer afford to care for them. This compelled me to petition my husband to adopt a second dog. A Pom/Chi mix, Ruthie came to us as her fourth try at a home in two years. She was not particularly well-trained or socialized, and she was slightly overweight. Nevertheless, Ruthie Pie has become the light of my husband's life and has firmly established herself as the happiest animal in the house. From the moment she wakes to when she falls asleep, she is such a goofy little dog that we can't help but smile at her. -*Jan E. Schmidt*

A New Breed of Best Friend

Born in a thunderstorm, he died gently in a snowstorm.

His downturn was fast and brief, a mere 24 hours. His vision was still as sharp as the red-tailed hawks' nesting high in the ancient cottonwood tree—the tree beneath which he would snuffle, carefully and slowly seeking out carrion fallen from the nest above. His ashes now circle that giant tree.

Almost deaf at the end, Rufus' fur was still thick, shining, and soft. At 73 pounds, he was down from his peak of 96 pounds and his fighting weight of 83 pounds. His massive chest and forequarters carried him forward through life with strength, power, and determination, although not through water. Several unplanned deep water experiences on the Negro Bill Trail in Moab, Utah, and in a lake at City Park in Denver, taught him never to venture deeper than he could stand or preferably lie down. He loved to lie in a stream flowing so swiftly he was almost swept away. Here, his massive chest was the dam upon which the white water would break, forming eddies back by his rump, his tail floating away downstream.

He had an illustrious career with skunk encounters; the last of five was on his 10th birthday in a culvert at Mary's Loop, Fruita, in western Colorado. He was blasted full force in the face by the sheltering skunk and spent the next half hour rubbing his face raw in the dirt. Finally, he succumbed to a decontamination treatment, and following a mountain bike ride with us, he was allowed in the car. His leather collar was another story. It spent the rest of the road trip slung around the passenger side mirror, and despite massive treatments, it soon met its fate in the dumpster.

Rufus had three run-ins with the law, all of which were misunderstandings. The worst was when he was heavily maced in Leadville, Colorado, protecting his "sister" Chutney and her cousin Leoncita when they were very young pups. A neighboring child had opened the garden gate, so the three dogs were on the front lawn where Rufus was watching over his young, playful charges. A postman was under the impression that he could walk onto the front lawn and not get deterred from fulfilling his duty. By all accounts, none of the dogs ever advanced toward the postman, yet he felt the need to call the dog catcher, who then maced Rufus to the state where he was completely incapacitated, lying in the gutter under my car—which is where we found him; the puppies were cowering under the car, hiding behind the fallen Rufus. My friend's intervention prevented my getting a felony charge for assaulting an officer, and all the government officials scattered quickly, sheepishly embarrassed at their overzealousness. The pups were none the worse for wear, but Rufus suffered massive eye rinses and face washings until the pepper spray was finally gone. Once again, he rubbed and rubbed his head in torment.

We discovered very early on that Rufus had a fetish: clean or dirty, but only socks. We left him in a hotel room during a quick dinner and returned to find all our socks strewn about the room, nary another item moved. There are many half-pairs of socks in our home and in the homes and wardrobes of forgetful friends. Rufus would steal them off chairs, out of drawers—anything was fair game, not just the floor. As he got bigger, he would swallow the sock, only for it to reappear a few days later, intact, out the other end. Sadly, they were never deemed ready for laundry after that...

Rufus was a road warrior, crisscrossing the country many times with us, but drive over a cattle grid or hit the rumble strips on the road and he completely fell apart, frantically trying to climb into my lap. (Did I mention his size?)

Our Boxer/Golden Retriever/Chow mix had traits and body parts from each breed. The funny thing was people insisted Rufus was a new breed they'd seen, which we discovered was usually a Belgian Malinois, even though he was twice their size. We became so fed up with people arguing with us about his pedigree that we decided he was actually a Polish Short-Haired Sable Hound. We told people about how this ancient breed hunted sable for its luxurious fur in the forests of Eastern Europe at the side of nobility...but that's a story unto itself.

Thriving for over 14½ years, Rufus' dignity, grace, courage, tenacity, mischievousness, loyalty, and stubbornness live on in us all.

 *Lowrey Mumford*

A Lesson in Forgiveness

We know little about Gracie's past, as she was picked up as a stray in the ghetto. She's a black Staffordshire Terrier who is somewhere between four and six years old, and she's practically blind. She had been used as a breeder and most likely kept outside during her young life. She was going to be euthanized because of her condition and the bad shape she was in, but a kind animal control officer contacted Hot Water Rescue in hopes that they could help her. The rescue took her in, had her spayed, and had her eyes checked because one was seriously bulging. She had a lot of scarring from bearing multiple litters of puppies. There were chew marks from her puppies on the sides of her face.

After a couple of months of TLC with her foster mom and some trips to the vet, Gracie is now in presentable condition and appears healthy and sound. We adopted her and took her to an ophthalmologist, but they weren't able to help her. It doesn't matter—we'll do all we can to make her comfortable and happy, even without great eyesight.

What we know for sure about Gracie is that she is lovable, kind, and anxious to please. Her greatest pleasure is lying next to us and having her belly rubbed. There is not one mean bone in her body. How this creature can be so lovable and trusting after what she has been through is truly amazing.

We brought Gracie into our home because we felt she needed a real home, where she could be loved and cared for, pampered and spoiled. She deserves that and will receive it for the rest of her life.

Although we have only had her for a short time, she has already surprised us by bringing much more comfort and love to us than we have given to her. She has a purpose in life—a real spirit—the capacity to love, trust, and obey. She has taught us the true meaning of forgiveness. Mankind has abused Gracie and tormented her, yet she has returned that torture with love and trust. What a lesson we have learned!

Those who think Pit Bulls are mean and dangerous should meet Gracie. And by the way, Gracie is not her full name. It is short for Amazing Gracie, a name we think is appropriate.

 *Irving Herskowitz*

The Smallest Star

As a volunteer at San Francisco Animal Care and Control, I get to know lots of dogs. I love them and do what I can to make their quality of life great.

A pregnant stray came into the shelter and had her four pups the first day. She was stressed and tense and exhibited protective behavior to keep her family safe, but snapping at the shelter staff made her look bad. I volunteered to foster her and her pups at my house until they were eight weeks old. At the time, they were three weeks old and had no teeth; they fit into my hand.

The mom was wary, but she liked my place better than the shelter. My boyfriend, Joe, and I got to name them. Tura, the fierce mom, we named after the actress Tura Satana from the movie *Faster Pussycat Kill Kill*, as she was a real tough girl. The little white-coated boy we named Jimmy after Jimmy McNulty of the show *The Wire*, and the girl pup we named Chloe because it was beautiful like she was. We named the little brown boy pup with the long coat Genghis, since he was the biggest and truly mighty, and we named the tiny boy Orion because his coat was a beautiful black-and-gray merle; it looked like the night sky.

Orion was not as loud or pushy as his siblings, and when they graduated to solid food, he wanted to stick with nursing. It was working well for him, and he would cuddle with his mom, nursing or not. While the other three were seeking out mischief and devilish play, Orion was just hanging out with his star—his mom.

Orion's siblings grew and grew, but he just seemed to stay small; they were eating a lot more than he was. We tried mixing wet food with puppy milk, puppy milk on its own, warming up the wet food, feeding him in a bowl, and feeding him by hand. He just wasn't into it. Tura was beginning to drive the babies away as they got bigger. She was weaning them, but Orion didn't want to give up nursing. He was truly a mama's boy.

One day Joe was holding Orion, talking to him in his low baritone voice and letting the puppy nuzzle his goatee. The feeling was right, and Orion began to eat wet food from Joe's hand. It was magic, and we were so happy. Joe was the main food provider for Orion during that time; they both liked the connection. When Joe, a normally tough and stoic guy, was cuddling and feeding Orion, he said, "Maybe we should think about adopting him."

I was concerned, since we already had a high-maintenance princess-of-a-German-Shepherd. Even though she got along very well with the puppies and their mom and had been a puppy mill mama dog in her past, I wasn't sure that adopting a puppy was the right choice. Joe and I went over the pros and cons as the puppies grew, and by the time they were eight weeks old, we were ready to adopt Orion. We realized we loved him so much there was just nothing else we could do.

Our good friends decided to adopt Orion's sister, and we were delighted. Before we knew it, we were saying goodbye to Tura and her pups and bringing little Orion back with us! The house is a blanket of dog toys, and he is a gorgeous and silly little guy. His relationship with our Shepherd, Shadow, is adorable; she is sometimes his friend and sometimes his strict German governess. We are a happy family and are currently enjoying puppy teeth dropping out of his mouth daily as his adult teeth come in.

Orion is doing great in his puppy classes and is a joy to have around. Now he eats like a champion, but he still has that sweet bond with Joe where he nuzzles his goatee and cuddles like he used to.

 *Erika Slovikoski*

Love and Acceptance

More than five years ago I was single and had just purchased my first home. I decided I needed a dog. There were a few problems, though. I was used to being transient, having lived in 11 locations and five states during the previous three years. I was selfish, having never given my undivided attention to anyone or anything. And I was unwilling to be vulnerable again because of prior baggage.

Although I was independent, I needed company. I told my friend that I was getting a dog to prepare me for marriage. She said, "You mean for kids?"

"No, marriage," I said. "I'm selfish and impatient and I think cleaning up his poop will prepare me for marriage."

"That's romantic," she teased. "You probably shouldn't tell that to the woman you marry."

I was serious, though. I thought having a dog would help break bad habits within me and teach me how to rely upon others. And since I was also frugal, I scoured the classifieds.

Like an expecting father, I had the name Rohan already picked out. I needed a burly, manly dog to fit the name, not a hold-in-the-palm-of-your-hands, needy dog. An ad in the local newspaper that read "Friendly Golden Retriever free to good home" led me to a big, handsome, bushy-haired Golden Retriever/Chow mix. He was a runaway mutt dumped in the country, but he was housebroken, about 18 months old, and highly active.

The lady behind the ad told me a sad story about how she saved him from euthanasia, but she needed to re-home him because she couldn't take care of two dogs. She let him slither out of the gate, and when she tried to switch collars on him, he streaked across the street like a lightning bolt. He peed on everything in sight and begged us to chase him. Ten minutes later we finally corralled him, and she asked me if I still wanted him. I said yes and loaded him into my SUV. He immediately threw his legs over the backseat and stared at me in the rearview mirror with deep, brown eyes as I drove home. And despite his apparent faults and the warnings that come with an unwanted dog, I was crazy about him already.

"Your name is Rohan," I told him. "Not that wussy name Goldberg she gave you after the professional wrestler."

I soon discovered that Rohan was rebellious, reckless, and free-spirited, but I would also learn that I needed him more than he needed me.

Rohan soon made my house his as fast as he could lift his leg, leaving his mark on everything from the fichus tree to the fireplace. He had severe ADHD, becoming distracted by a bird chirping in Australia or a dog barking three states away. He tunneled out of the back yard numerous times and killed three trees: two by urination and one by digging it up. He tore a book to shreds. He stole bubble gum from my bag and food from the counter. He tipped his bowls over hundreds of times when lonely, and his bowels occasionally moved when home alone for even short periods of time. On top of all that, he had been abused in his younger years and was dog aggressive toward even harmless dogs.

I tried to exercise the energy out of Rohan, but he always had energy. He nearly yanked my arm out of the socket on runs. I tied him to my bicycle and rode him around the neighborhood for a while until one afternoon a cat darted in front of us, and he flipped the bike, sending me to the pavement. I slammed into a fence on rollerblades because he didn't want to turn when I did.

But because of Rohan, I changed tremendously as a person, and I got married three years later. Two years into our marriage, my wife suggested we begin a family. We tried to have a baby, but we faced numerous fertility problems and endured two miscarriages. Needing to nurture something, we decided to bring a puppy home. Rohan wasn't having it, though, and we had a decision to make. Despite loving Rohan, my wife wanted the puppy. She needed the puppy.

I contacted multiple dog trainers, and only one said she "may" be able to break him of his aggression, but it would take lots of time, effort, and money. I called the humane society to see if they could find Rohan a home. "Not with his past," the man answered. "You need to give away the puppy, or bring your dog in here, hold him, and tell him you love him while we put him to sleep."

I shed tears at the thought of putting him down and life without him. Our bond became stronger and his loyalty impeccable after that.

But I wanted to break this old dog of his dog aggression. And that's how he died: me trying to exercise and socialize him beyond what he could handle. I took him to the local dog park on a warm afternoon because we could only go when there were fewer dogs. He had a great time for about 25 minutes, chasing the other dogs along the fence line, but once we arrived home, he wobbled dizzily. I hurried him to the back yard and hosed him off for 20 minutes. I petted him and told him I needed him to hang on and fight. Then, something snapped in his mind, and I watched him transform from my fun-loving, energetic, big-kid-at-heart to a scared, fighting for life, blind, incoherent dog who passed on about 12 hours later at the emergency clinic.

My regular vet recorded his temperature at 109 and said most dogs rarely survive for longer than a few hours once their body temperature reaches 107. With tears streaking down my cheeks, I petted him and tried to talk him back into his former self, and he communicated with me through a round of weak, raspy barks, despite not being able to see me. I left for a few hours to regroup, and the vet techs said he whined the whole time I was gone. We transported him to the emergency clinic, and he fought through the night, but the next morning he had cardiac arrest and passed on.

My wife and I can laugh with tears about him now, but we have come to realize that he was really an awful pet. The previous, selfish me, would have taken the easy way out and never worked through his numerous faults. But the new me, the one who learned how to love because of an unwanted, runaway mutt, didn't have the heart to see anything bad happen to him. And that's the thing about loving someone or something unconditionally: You accept their faults and love them anyway. Our house will always feel empty without Rohan, and so will a piece of my heart.

 *Ryan Barnhart*

A Tail of Many Pages

I remember exactly when my mom called and gave us the news that Rosie, the dog from the humane society of whom I'd only heard stories of from mom, was ours. Dad took us straight to Mom's house with my little brother, Rhys, still struggling with his shoes.

I opened the car door before it stopped moving completely. Rhys, always one for caution, got out with my dad after the car was parked.

A medium, not huge, but certainly not small dog, her main color being brown, but with a white nose and belly, was trying to lick my mom's face, while jumping all over her.

"Chaos! That dog looks absolutely chaotic!" That was my first thought.

My second thought was, "Don't judge a book by its cover."

Why did I think of that? That saying was probably invented 10 thousand years ago, in Ancient Egypt or something. But I guess it was true. I mean, I didn't even know this dog.

I ran over to my mom, and even though I really wanted to see what book Rosie was (a good one?), I gave my mom a hug. I had just seen her the day before.

Rosie, apparently, had different plans for us. She jumped on us and whimpered like crazy! Finally, I leaned down, to pet her, and she lay down and licked my face.

Rosie, now more commonly called Dog, Rose, Rosebud, or Sweetheart, is a loving book, a good-intentions-that-usually-turn-out-a-bit-wrong book, a funny book, a lazy but very energetic book, and an always-by-your-side book. I'm glad I didn't judge her by her "cover," or I may have never opened the book and found all the wonderful things inside it.

 *Hannah Davey, Age 10*

Man in a Lamb Suit

Our lovely, little man-in-a-lamb-suit, Crawford, is a Golden Retriever/Poodle mix, a.k.a. "golden doodle." His story began in a puppy mill, where he was crated and then cast aside to live his very early months with older male and female breeding dogs on the last legs of their "usefulness." These sweet creatures were vulnerable to occasional BB shots from neighboring teenagers, and the cacophony of canine panic was the most constant noise to this young puppy's ears. What food he was given was wolfed down. He slept where he pottied. Feral fear was his only companion, and his social sense was one of anxiety when a human approached. Pacing his small area and beating his little boney tail against the sides of his cage became his only gesture of reacting to his desperate world of hunger, loneliness, and filth.

Crawford's inclusion on a rescue truck from GRRAND, the Golden Retriever Rescue in Louisville, Kentucky, was a fortunate accident and a miracle. He was placed in the rescue truck with 12 older breeding Goldens, and when delivered by GRRAND volunteers, he had to be carried off the truck because his fear would not let him move. This matted and urine-soaked "mop" was gently laid on the pavement, as the GRRAND volunteers marveled at his inclusion with these older Goldens.

Before going into foster care, Crawford would not walk. Volunteers gently placed towels around his belly to hoist him up and encourage him. The rescue washed and vetted him, and then Crawford made his way into foster care and onto the GRRAND adoption website. His foster mom has two GRRAND Goldens and was present when the puppy mill rescue truck arrived. Crawford became her charge, and his little, damaged tail became her challenge, as Crawford had beaten it raw and bloody from anxiety and frustration. Developing Crawford's social skills and finding a forever home became his foster mom's quest. She groomed him and slowly taught him the kindness of touch from a human hand.

This is where the Wilt Family came into Crawford's tale. We had recently moved to Louisville from Ohio and had some experience with an older rescue puppy mill brood Labrador: the gorgeous Lolabelle, who had been literally dumped in the night pen at a local shelter in our Ohio town. Lola was severely diabetic and going blind when we got her. Our move to Kentucky really pointed out the blindness as she was increasingly disoriented. Steve and I discovered that her cataracts could be removed to correct her sight, and while she had other health issues, we both felt that she deserved this one last gift from us. We took her to the vet to get the testing and surgery. One of Steve's best memories is of Lolabelle walking down the hall with her eye surgeon. She could see his face and associated it with his voice for the first time. There was pure joy in her smile. She improved with her sight and enjoyed the love of her pack. Despite our efforts and 48 units of Vetsulin a day, she did pass. Our only comfort was that Lola finished BIG. She passed knowing that she was loved.

The rest of our canine pack was in mourning, obviously confused and searching our home for her. The Wilt Family is a blended one—all of us are "steps" or adopted in one way or another—and the loss of one of our family, especially when so much effort is put into inclusion, is especially heartfelt. Our belles, Clarabelle (yellow Labrador), Nelliebelle (Golden), and Jezebelle (Great Dane), were the rhythm of our home. And because we all had loved Lola so dearly, there was a sense, almost like a message from her, that we could honor her memory by making room for another dog in need.

I had heard about GRRAND and applied for adoption, never knowing who or what we would face. Crawford's picture came on our radar and seized our hearts. So very shy, he came for an introductory walk with our pack of canines. Wrapped around the legs of his foster mom, he spun and balked and shied away from treats or toys. Crawford took the full measure of us, and he was not so sure. His little tail was taped up, and it was that little tail of won us over. Hanging between his legs, that tail called out for care, as if to say, "Would you please love me?"

Most importantly, it needed to wag.

Crawford's foster mom was also convinced. Crawford had found his forever home.

Where does that moment occur when there is acceptance of love? For us, we just saw need and entered the trials of rehabilitation right away. Crawford had to learn to love and trust us at his own pace, which was slow and frustrating. But what we have learned from helping Crawford acclimate into our pack is the uniqueness of every dog's spirit. Dogs don't lie about love or pack acceptance.

Crawford has brought both challenge and pure happiness to our lives. He has grown into his confidence and has developed a full wooly coat of white curls, causing the nickname "little man in a lamb suit." A tiny football is his favorite toy, chasing it his favorite play. His best friend is a rather large Great Dane named Jezebelle, who is as bold as Crawford is shy. She's the lion our lamb needed. And Crawford's tail? It flies!

 *The Wilt Family*

Trust Takes Time

The crazy cat lady—every neighborhood has one. In my neighborhood, she appeared to be *me*. Throughout my adult life, I have owned quite a few cats. I never wanted a dog. It's not that I disliked dogs; I was more or less indifferent to them. But then I met my neighbor's Australian Shepherd. She was sweet and loveable, and we were smitten with each other. One day I actually had a startling thought cross my mind: If I ever owned a dog—which I knew I wouldn't—I would want my dog to be just like her.

One day I found myself looking at dogs on Petfinder.com. No big deal, I was "just looking." I already had four cats; what would I do with a dog? But my sporadic browsing became a semi-regular habit. I was looking at Aussies. Wouldn't every Aussie be like my neighbor's dog? I was looking at young dogs, not puppies. I was looking at medium-sized dogs, not small and not large dogs. Before I knew it, browsing through Petfinder. com became almost a daily routine, yet still I had no serious intentions. But then one day it happened—I saw Mindy.

Mindy's picture struck a chord in me. What a precious face, and those pretty brown puppy-dog eyes! The words **URGENT** and **SAVE A LIFE** practically jumped out at me through the computer screen. A young Australian Shepherd-mix—just what I was looking for! I called my husband over to the computer and showed him Mindy. He asked if I wanted to go see her at the shelter, which was about 30 miles from our house, and I quickly said, "Oh no, I was just looking... She is *so* cute though... Well, it can't hurt to just go look... What if we drive all the way down there, and she is gone?"

Once we arrived at the shelter, we set out to find Mindy. I thought she would be easy to spot since we had her picture in hand, but we didn't see her. Looking past the other dogs, who were barking at us and trying so hard to get our attention, was heart-wrenching, but our mission was to find Mindy. Finally, mixed between all the dogs excitedly jumping up and down, we saw this meek-looking dog standing still and staring at us without an iota of excitement. I looked at the print out, and I looked at her. The markings were the same, but it wasn't quite the cherubic face as was in the picture. Instead, staring at us was a face full of sadness and fear attached to a body that was too thin with scraggly fur. There she stood—we had found Mindy.

Mindy moved very slowly and appeared timid and nervous. She looked young, still very much like a puppy. We did not get much of a background story on her, other than that she was owner surrendered and pregnant when she was arrived at a different shelter. Once she had her puppies, she was transferred to this particular shelter because it could accommodate her and the pups better. We were informed that she exhibited nervous behavior, especially around men, so it was pretty certain that she had been mistreated in some fashion. I asked if she was good around cats and was told they didn't know for sure, but she seemed fine when she walked by them in the vet's office. She didn't act aggressively toward them.

I wish I could say that I felt an instantaneous love for her, but it was hard when she was so withdrawn. Still, I saw something deep in her eyes that started to overwhelm me, and I had an emotional breakthrough. This dog has been through so much in her short life. She was sent away from her home for whatever reason (which was for the best if she had been mistreated). She had babies, and they were taken away from her, one by one, while she stood by and watched, and now she was all alone. She had every right to be scared and sad. With so many emotions tugging at my heartstrings, I muttered to my husband, "I think I want her."

What did I just say? My head was whirling, and my brain was on information overload. I mean, I didn't want a dog, right? I didn't even know what to do with a dog! I already had four cats. Cats are easy. What was I going to do with a dog?

Adapting to her new home was a huge adjustment for Mindy. Her nervous tendencies were almost crippling, but we continued to be patient with her, hoping that she would come around. I will never forget the first time she dropped her guard around me. I took her into the back yard, called her name, and playfully ran towards her. She perked up and actually pounced a little with excitement before quickly returning to her submissive stance. For me, it was a monumental occasion. I felt a warm sensation come over me; my eyes welled up with happiness. Why did it affect me this way? Because I knew that it had happened. I was completely in love with my dog.

 *Dawn Starek*

More than a Mascot

People associate Dalmatians with fire trucks, often thinking of them as a mascot, but Sparkles, my Dalmatian who was rescued from a home with 62 other dogs before coming to live with me, is so much more. She is an active role model and a fire safety teacher for young children. Sparkles is never happier than when she wears her red vest and shiny red badge. She loves sharing the fire safety message with children.

My focus of helping save young children from fire came soon after I became a volunteer firefighter. I found out that children under the age of five account for the largest number of fatalities from fire: 11%, and I wanted to do something to reduce this unfortunate statistic. I could not have asked for a more amazing partner to help me on this mission.

When Sparkles was younger, we'd practice fire safety. She would jump into her bed, and I would cover her with a blanket. She would pretend to be asleep. As the smoke alarm sounded, she would jump out of bed, crawl low, and go to her meeting place. The above became a very effective way of reinforcing the fire safety behaviors taught by firefighters.

I'll never forget a visit two years ago to Celia Clinton Elementary School in Tulsa, Oklahoma, to read our book, *Sparkles the Fire Safety Dog,* and make a fire safety presentation to approximately 450 students. Each child that day received a free copy of our book, compliments of Tulsa Rotary Club.

The following January I received a telephone call from the Celia Clinton Elementary School principal. She told me that two of her students were involved in separate fire situations over the holidays, but they knew what to do to get their families out of their homes safely because of the lessons Sparkles taught them.

I sat there quietly, soaking in the principal's words; I was totally speechless. Tears streamed down my face; I could not believe what I was hearing. It became clear to me this was a teachable moment and that Sparkles and I needed to go back to Celia Clinton to visit the children and reinforce fire safety. I could not wait to meet those who had helped save their families. The event was an emotional one for me, and I try to hold back the tears each time I share the story.

During the return visit to Celia Clinton, five-year-old Angelica shared the following with me: "Firefighter Dayna, I was in bed under the cobers and the smoke came. I crawled out of bed and crawled low, just like Sparkles showed me to.

I said, 'C'mon daddy, you have to get on the floor and crawl low like Sparkles.'"

By this time, Angelica's dad had become disoriented because he had been standing in the smoke-filled room. Thankfully, he was able to follow Angelica out of the house. The firefighters later shared with me that as soon as Angelica's father reached the door, they scooped him up and took him to the hospital, where he spent seven days, four of which were in intensive care. The firefighters also mentioned that the home flashed over just as they got Angelica's dad to the threshold of the door. (A "flashover" occurs when the home becomes totally engulfed in flames.)

A day does not go by when I do not think of Angelica and her story. I am so thankful that she and her dad are safe, and I am humbled knowing that the fire safety presentation Sparkles and I made helped save their lives.

Sparkles has helped firefighters reach millions of children and their caregivers with the fire safety message since I adopted her seven years ago. Now that she is older and does not travel as much anymore, we offer Skype visits with schools throughout the United States and abroad. Especially because of budget cuts, Skype visits have become a perfect way to share the fire safety message. They also allow us to reach children all over the world.

Every day Sparkles is in my life she is a blessing. When I think about all the lives she has touched throughout the years, I realize just how lucky I am. Not only is she an amazing fire safety dog and a true credit to the fire service, she is a wonderful friend and companion.

 *Dayna Hilton*

Jake's Best Friends

This is a story that I have to write because I can't stand telling it without crying. My nephew, Jake, was a young man who loved his mixed-breed dogs, Belle River and Molson. Belle is a Border Collie-mix, and Molson is a Lab-mix. The dogs went with Jake everywhere.

It was a cold, snowy, and windy night in Michigan when Jake was on his way home from a friend's house. As Jake came up over an incline, he lost control of his truck. It's believed that he hit a spot of black ice.

Jake's truck went into the median and rolled over, causing Jake and the dogs to be ejected from the truck. A witness that was behind Jake's truck said that he spotted two dogs running across the highway and thought that maybe Jake had rolled his truck while trying to avoid the dogs, which he assumed had caused the accident. But that wasn't the case; the dogs were Belle River and Molson.

The witness stopped and put his and his wife's coats on Jake, and Belle River came back after a short while to wait by Jake's side. When the police arrived, they put Belle in their car to take her to a shelter. Jake died that night on the highway with Belle beside him.

As his family mourned their loss, they also worried about what had happened to Molson. Jake's sister Christine went to the underpass where the accident happened and walked around looking for Molson. Friends of Jake's also looked and stopped at houses in the area, asking if anyone had seen a black dog. Some had seen her, and one man in particular had tried to coax her to him. She was so frightened and cold she ran instead. Chris and Jake's friends saw tracks that looked like they could be Molson's. How could she survive in this terribly cold weather when she was used to being in the warm comfort of a home? Day after day Chris made the trip out to the area, not knowing what else to do.

After a few days, a friend told Christine that her father was a hunter, and if he ever lost track of a dog, he would leave his coat on the ground. Sometimes the dog would come back to it. Christine was willing to try anything, so she took the comforter off Jake's bed that very day and put it outside where Molson was last seen, under the highway where Jake had died. Chris left her phone number with the man who lived nearby and had seen Molson.

The next morning the phone rang, and it was the man who had been seeing our Molson. He told Christine that he believed Molson was there by the blanket. Christine left right away, and when she arrived, she found Molson sitting on the blanket, waiting for Jake to return. Molson spotted Christine and recognized her, so she was able to hug Molson and tell her everything would be alright.

Jake's mom had picked up Belle River from the shelter, and now Molson would make his home with Christine, her husband, Dennis, and their dog, Miette. Molson has had a good life with Christine even though we're sure she still thinks of Jake. Belle River has been Janice's (Jake's mom) constant companion and has also had a terrific life. They are much loved dogs.

 *Linda Beals*

Training the Un-trainable

S kylo was our first adopted dog and probably the smartest dog I have met. A 13-month-old Husky/Basenji mix from the SPCA, he was a supposed escape artist who couldn't be kept by numerous owners. He was also at the end of his rope—this was a time when animals were put down if unadoptable instead of the current method of networking with other cities' shelters and shipping pets to where they are wanted. Fortunately for us, a softhearted staff member had prolonged this as long as he could, which turned out to be just long enough.

We were living quite secluded in the bush at the time and had the ability to give Skylo the space to run and get it out of his system. Of course, there were times when he still ran away after a deer or rabbit, but when he got home, we would ostracize him by ignoring him and leaving him alone for at least an hour. It was the worst thing he could undergo, and when we finally released him, he was so happy to please it was comical! This method works better than any punishment could to teach an animal you are displeased with their actions, for any pack animal knows it is like a death sentence to be kicked out of the pack.

We also developed a trick: When walking in the forest, we would hide or reverse our direction on Skylo when he wandered ahead, and he soon learned that to be close to us he had to pay attention all the time. It didn't take long for us to be inseparable. Skylo eventually became a perfect companion, learning more than 30 verbal commands as well as the hand signs to accompany them.

Skylo learned to run to us when he spotted a deer rather than giving chase. On more than one occasion, he treed a bear to protect my wife, Lillian, from harm and would not relent until she was safely down the trail, where he would proudly join her. Sadly we lost Skylo to a speeding driver on our street, and despite the pain of losing such a good friend, we honored Skylo's friendship by adopting another dog who desperately needed a home.

 *Dave Brummet*

She was a very sad-looking White German Shepherd lying at the back of a run, underweight with the fur above her hips shaved off and some of her bones showing through. The sign on the kennel door said "Not for Adoption." Not knowing much about how shelters worked at the time, I assumed someone had either come to adopt her or the owner had claimed her and would be arriving shortly.

I decided to take her out of her cage while I waited for the other members of our rescue group to arrive. She had a quiet dignity about her, tentatively approaching me as I opened the door to her run. Outside of her run, there was a grassy area, and since no dogs were out, I let her run around without holding onto her leash. She did a couple funny bunny hops, keeping both rear legs in unison when she walked. After spending some time with her, I struck up a conversation with one of the shelter workers, and I was shocked to find out the reason she was "Not for Adoption."

Apparently the police found her limping near the shelter and brought her in. They assumed that she had been hit by a car. Shelters in New Jersey are required by the state to hold a stray dog for seven days, after which they can put the dog down. She had been there for six days. Since she was around 11 years old, and the shelter did not have the resources to take care of her; they were going to put her to sleep on Monday.

Having had a White German Shepherd as a child, I was naturally attracted to her, but there was still something special; a gentle yet stoic presence. After some arm-twisting and emotional arguments with my wife, I told the shelter that I would return on Tuesday to adopt her.

The ensuing vet visit found no evidence of an accident or blunt trauma to her hips, back, or legs. The vet found fleas, severe arthritis, and the beginnings of degenerative myelopathy, where the rear paws start to knuckle under and the tops scrape and bleed. I bought her booties help prevent the scrapes and neglected to tell the friend whose van I borrowed to pick her up about the fleas. All things considered, she was in better shape than I could have hoped. At first I wanted to name her Phoenix, but my wife felt that didn't really match her personality, so we named her Sedona.

I spent the first few nights downstairs on the couch while Sedona curled against the wall in our den. I had to approach her slowly; she was still cautious about her new setting and sometimes turned and hopped around our dining room table. After a week she tentatively began to come up to me for attention. Eventually she greeted me at the door when I came home and followed me around the house, though always a foot or so behind me.

Amazingly, instead of progressively getting worse, she became stronger in her hind legs and put on about 10 pounds. We took her for sessions of acupuncture and put her on Rimadyl, a non-steroidal anti-inflammatory drug for dogs. While she had no interest in chasing balls, she was tireless on her walks. Within a year, we went to the reservation for an hour walk. She would slowly fall behind me, then catch up, then fall behind. Five minutes after we came home, she would be at the door, looking up, ready to go back out for a walk.

Despite her age, arthritis, and other joint problems, she kept plugging along. About two years after she came to us, she got bloat and we rushed her to the emergency vet in Red Bank, NJ. At this point she was close to 13, she had slowed down considerably, and we were taking her for water therapy to try to maintain muscle mass. Even if she made it through the surgery, it would be tough road. My wife and I were prepared to not go through with the surgery, but when the vet wheeled her in on a gurney for us to say goodbye, despite the medication in her system, she looked at us and tried to get up. We knew she wasn't ready to quit. The surgery was successful.

The last few months were difficult for me. Though shy and timid to everyone she first met, Sedona was always by my side, and perhaps because I was too close to the situation, I didn't see how she would never give up around me. I was away one weekend, and when I came home, my wife said Sedona didn't want to go out and wouldn't go past the end block on her walk, which was so different from when I was around. Whenever she was with me, Sedona kept going. My wife said, "You don't see it, but she will do anything for you. When you are here, she is a different dog." All dog owners know the end is never easy. Dogs trust us to be their guardians and make the difficult choice.

The last month we had Sedona, she had a favorite spot: the back of our old Honda. She would lie in the back seat for hours comfortable and content, looking around while we worked outside. There is no true way to describe how she told me it was time, except to say there was a look of acceptance that no more could be done. The next day we took her to our vet and stayed with her in the back of the car until the end. We had her for two years and seven months, and she is always with me in spirit.

 *James C. Dascoli*

Doggie Doings

A Clear Message: Chloe came to live with us last year after my friend had to give up her home and sadly, her dog. Then, this past spring I transported two Min Pins, Rhett and Scarlette, from Kansas City to Colorado for my friend Harold. They both stayed with us for a week until I had to go back out on the road, at which time they went to stay with my parents. Harold came to pick them up two days later. Rhett went with Harold rather willingly, but Scarlette made known that she wanted to stay...by *biting* Harold! My dad told Harold to leave her with them for the time being, but when Harold returned a few weeks later and tried to take Scarlette with him, she again let him know she wasn't interested. While all this was going on, Chloe was just chewing her nails because she didn't like Scarlette getting *her* attention. Finally, Harold showed up when I was home. I couldn't believe that when he tried to get Scarlette to come to him, Chloe growled at him! That's when we decided to keep Scarlette. Now her and Chloe are thick as thieves.
-Tom Beard

Say Hi, Small Fry: My husband didn't want a dog, but I created a whole campaign to change his mind. Every day I would send him photos of dogs needing homes, and finally one little dog caught his attention. Small Fry, a Pom/Eskimo mix, was ours from the moment he curled up in my husband's lap. Today Small Fry plays with two cats and moves my slippers around the house. He is my baby and very spoiled. When friends come to visit, we have to check their coats or purses to make sure they are not smuggling Small Fry out of our house. He is definitely Mr. Popular, in addition to being an avid squirrel chaser! *-Jan E. Schmidt*

Sea-Level Saints

Over the past few years, my wife, Karan, and I have fallen in love with the Caribbean tri-island nation of Grenada. When most Americans think of Grenada, they think of a tiny island country somewhere in the Caribbean that the U.S. military invaded sometime in the mid 1980's to overthrow a militant Marxist government gone awry and to save the American students attending medical school on the island. This is all true, but Grenada is so much more. Grenada, nicknamed the Spice Isle, grows some of the most delicious spices ever tasted: nutmeg, cinnamon, clove, ginger, and cocoa, just to name a few. Grenada's lush, green, high-mountain rainforest teems with towering picturesque waterfalls cascading forth into clear, fast-running streams that flow through valleys and villages down to the sea. It is Grenada's beaches, bays, and turquoise blue sea that brings yachters and tourists from around the world and maybe one day will bring you, too. But our story isn't so much about Grenada; it's about Grenada's dogs, or should I say, a most specific dog of the Spice Isle.

One day Karan and I were walking along the Caranage of St. George's Harbour, one of the most renowned and busiest places in Grenada. In a back alley, just off the busy street and sidewalk, we saw the saddest dog we had ever seen: a black-and-brown female dog: her sunken-in, deformed body not much more than a living skeleton of protruding bones and sagging, long-ago depleted nipples. The dog's bony hips and lower back were crooked and bent, broken not too long before from being bounced (hit) by a car. Each of the pitiful dog's bony hindquarters was one huge scab from the dog being tied up on a two- or three-foot chain all her life, having only rough concrete to sit and lie upon, most likely without any shade. It was obvious by looking at the emaciated dog that she was provided little, if any, food and water.

The sick, pitiful dog was in the alley half-sitting, half-standing—uncomfortable either way—drinking from a tiny pool of dirty water, which had gathered in a crack in the concrete from a dirty dripping pipe. I immediately went to a nearby grocery store and bought some dog food while Karan cared for the dog. As I watched the starving dog pick at the food, her starvation so severe that her hunger had long ago gone, Karan talked on the telephone to a government animal control officer, who gave us the telephone number of the GSPCA (Grenada Society of the Prevention of Cruelty to Animals).

As Karan spoke with Peggy, the director of the GSPCA, I squatted down and gave the poor dog some pets. When I finished petting her, the starving dog placed her small black head in my hands and lifted her face, her soft brown eyes gazing soulfully into mine. To Karan's happy surprise, the GSPCA was a no-kill shelter. Peggy told us to bring the dog to the shelter, which was not far from the Caranage, and put her in the fenced-in side yard. She said she would care for the dog in the morning; for it was a Friday evening, and Peggy was in another town on the other side of the island.

Karan flagged down a taxi van, whose driver said he would take us to the shelter if we put the dog in a box. Karan quickly found a large cardboard box, but we weren't sure if a dog this hurt, starved, and mistreated dog would allow us to pick her up and put her in it. Much to our amazement, the severely abused stray did not snap or fidget or try to get away in the very least. Finally feeling loved for the first time in her abused life, she let Karan pick her up and put her in the cardboard box as if it were a soft bed. The taxi driver quickly drove us the few blocks from the Caranage, up a short, very steep hill to the GSPCA, where we put the dog in the fenced-in yard. We filled a nearby bowl with water and poured out some dog food, leaving the small bag of dog food open beside it. We set up the cardboard box as if it were a dog house, which the sick dog immediately took advantage of for a nap.

First thing the next morning, we received a call from the Peggy. She was at the animal shelter, but there was no dog. She had telephoned all the local members about the dog, thinking one of them might have taken her home to care for her. But no one knew about the dog. Peggy said she was going to look for her and would call us back.

A half hour or so later, we received a call. Peggy told us that as she was walking down the steep hill from the shelter to the Caranage, she saw the ill, exhausted black-and-brown dog walking up the hill to the shelter. The dog had a thin nylon leash with the shelter's name on it tied around her neck, which she had bitten through.

Peggy believed the taxi driver knew the owner of the dog, which is sadly amazing that a dog owner could and would allow their dog to literally starve to death. The owner, for some reason, had gone to the animal shelter and had taken the dog (along with the dog food) back to his or her house. He or she had tied the dog up with the very short leash taken from the yard of the animal shelter. During the early morning, when everyone was asleep and the Caranage was quiet, the dog had chewed through the leash and was making her way back to the shelter where she knew she would be loved, even though the dog had never seen a single person there.

The people at the animal shelter instantly fell in love with the dog and named her Kiki. For the shelter's staff, Kiki is a miracle dog who found a loving home after being fixed and fattened.

What's in Granada? Besides the calming waters, there are loving homes, loving families, and a loving shelter that unconditionally took in a starving, unwanted, and uncared for dog and transformed her into everyone's beloved Kiki.

 *Jack Russell*

Eddy Makes Waves

Sitting down with a nice steak and baked potato one night, I decided to read my emails over dinner. One was about a Boston Terrier in a high-kill shelter—nothing unusual there, I figured—but I read on. Then I saw a photo of dear Eddington, a Boston Terrier/Boxer mix with all of his ribs sticking out. I dropped my fork, and all I could think was, "Oh, my dear God, where is this poor dog?"

I called the president of the rescue group with whom I volunteered and emailed frantically, trying to figure out how to get Eddington out of the shelter. I wanted him at my house, now, but he was in Maryland, and I live in New York. Luckily we found someone to pull him from the shelter, and then we had to make transportation arrangements...fast.

And we did. Eddington was soon with me after staying with a great new foster mom near the shelter. We have a deli, which is where we started cooking madly for Eddington, cobbling together all the calories and fat and protein we could find. We portioned it all up and started hourly feedings mixed with rest and walks and tons of water. By day three we saw less ribs and more floppy, goofy dog.

As we rehabilitated Eddington, our deli customers dropped off food and towels and treats for him by the basket-full. I even had a friend and customer take him for an overnight at the lake, so I could sleep a little. Between the hourly feedings and the other Bostons—five to be exact—I was too pooped to even function. I gladly found myself cooking to-go meals for him as friends helped me care for him.

Eddington is a *big* baby now and on his way to a speedy recovery. Oh, and that steak and potato I was eating the first night I heard of him? I put them in the fridge, so they could be his first meal. I know sweet Eddy will find a forever home soon, but I hope not too soon because I love to see him bouncing around and trying to get everyone's attention, especially now that I no longer lie awake at night counting his ribs and petting him.

Jill Cook

Best of the West

Dogs have always been a part of our families. Even before Monique and I were married, we both had fond memories of our childhood dogs and dogs who shared our early adulthood. We each brought rescued dogs into our marriage four years ago. The Outlaw Josey Wales, a Black Lab-mix with an attitude and a heart of gold, was rescued from the Denver Dumb Friends League. Bailey Bear, a Golden Retriever with an incredibly loyal, jovial personality, was rescued from a struggling Phoenix family.

Our pups (no matter what their ages, they remain pups) had never shared their owners or homes with another dog before my wife and I married, but they adjusted well. There were a few incidents early on when they were establishing dominance, but they quickly became inseparable. Daily walks, weekend trips to the bark park, camping trips, and incredible hikes were shared among all members of our family. Like brothers, the dogs ate, slept, sniffed, and even barked in unison.

Monique and I were blessed with our first son, Brody, two years ago. Josey and Bailey were obviously curious but welcomed Brody into our home. Our lives changed, but Monique and I remained committed to not reducing the importance of our dogs in our lives. The pups continued to enjoy all they previously had with their new family member in tow.

Tragically, about a month after Brody's birth, we noticed a growth on Bailey's abdomen. Many vet appointments and specialists later, it was diagnosed as a benign, regionalized tumor, and we decided to have it removed surgically at Colorado State University's nationally recognized veterinary school. Surgery was a success, but it was later discovered that the cancer may have spread. We were devastated, but Bailey seemed committed to fight, so how couldn't we?

Several treatments of chemo followed, and his health began successively getting worse. He remained a loyal, happy pup, even when it was obvious that he was struggling. Josey sensed that Bailey wasn't well and gave him space and love. Somehow Josey knew they couldn't wrestle or run together like they used to, but Josey still wanted to be close.

Sadly, Bailey Bear passed one beautiful morning in February after valiantly fighting for six months. The cancer had moved to his lungs and made breathing increasingly difficult. On the last day, Bailey walked into the clinic like a dignified pup and wagged his tail just because he was around us. Monique, Brody, and I were in the veterinary emergency room with him while he lay on his dog bed from home.

The choking and heavy breathing had gotten worse over the past couple days and left him with peaceful 5- to 45-minute stretches between painful gasping sessions as he just tried to draw breath. The euthanasia serum was administered while he lay peacefully on his bed between us. It was tough watching Bailey draw his last breath after giving us so much and knowing he would have so much more to give if it hadn't been for the cancer. We took our strength from our memories of him and the knowledge that he was going to a happier place where he could eternally chase tennis balls and swim.

Josey sensed our sadness upon our return home and seemed to equally mourn Bailey for several months. Nothing was the same without him; we missed Bailey in everything we did.

We knew we wanted another Golden but didn't know when. Several months passed before we decided to begin our search. We applied and were accepted through several Golden rescue organizations, but the timing never seemed right. One Monday Monique surprised me with information that Petco was sponsoring an adopt-a-thon the following Saturday. Golden Retriever Freedom Rescue of Colorado (GRFR) was there, and we were pre-approved. Excitement built throughout the week, and I knew there was no way we would be walking away Saturday without a new Golden in tow.

We arrived open-minded, but Wyatt quickly found us and captivated us with his free spirit and loving ways. Several pups courted us, but Wyatt always snuck back into the picture. It quickly became clear that this two-year-old was joining our family, and Josey seemed to approve.

The only drawback to adopting an older pup is that you never see how cute they were as puppies. However, this small negative is quickly overshadowed by the joy a rescued pup shows upon finding out he is going to a new home. Wyatt latched himself to us that morning and has been an amazing addition to our family ever since.

Wyatt had been introduced to us as Atilla, but the name didn't fit such a well-mannered pup. We decided we wanted a western name to match the Outlaw Josey Wales. Poor Wyatt was called several names before settling on Wyatt Gatlin (every pup needs a middle name). Although he isn't quiet, we gave Wyatt the nickname Quiet Wyatt based on the 80's rock band.

We almost felt guilty about how easily Wyatt assimilated into our family: no accidents or chewed baby toys. Somebody had loved this pup, and somehow we were blessed to adopt him. Josey Wales and Quiet Wyatt quickly became buddies and wrestling partners. Wyatt adapted to the rhythms of our house, and we thought he could do no wrong. That feeling lasted for about eight hours. Monique and I are trying to sell our house, so we keep it extra-clean. As we sat on the patio eating dinner, we witnessed Quiet Wyatt's love for sprinklers. Wyatt chased the water streaming from each head until every hair on his body was waterlogged. He then dashed into the house through the dog door and shook every ounce of water from his body. We now water the lawn in the middle of the night.

While Goldens have similar qualities, not all have similar personalities. Incredibly, Wyatt seems to have many of Bailey's personality traits. They both are good on a leash but quick to run and explore given the chance. Both will jump in any water and actually sit in a running stream. Like Bailey, Wyatt will chase a ball until he is absolutely exhausted; then he will ask for more. Most importantly Wyatt, like Bailey, loves his family and is extremely tender around Brody and other children.

Josey is happy to have a partner, and we can't help but feel very fortunate to have such an amazing pup in our lives. It would not have been possible to seamlessly bring another pup into our lives without incredible organizations like GRFR. Rescued dogs will always be part of our family.

 *John Leber*

Silver Paws for Golden People

Amelia came into my life 2½ years ago through the Silver Paws program of Atlanta Animal Rescue Friends (AARF). I had recently gone through a divorce, and my life was very empty. I have always loved dogs and had hoped to have one again someday. I saw an article in the paper about AARF, which mentioned the Silver Paws program. What a great idea: rescuing senior dogs and placing them with senior people. "Mature" dog lovers could become Silver Paws foster parents, which meant becoming a permanent caretaker for an elderly dog without the financial burden of veterinary bills and the like. I thought, "Count me in!"

After my application was reviewed and a volunteer completed a home visit, I was approved as a foster home.

When I was notified about Amelia, an 11-year-old German Shepherd who needed a home, I was very excited! She had been living at a vet clinic for a couple of months after her owners had to give her up. The clinic staff thought one reason she hadn't been adopted was because of her age. In reality it was probably several factors: her age, breed, size, and the fact that she is almost all black.

It only took one weekend to bond with Amelia, and now it's like we've been together for years. Amelia has brought so much joy into my life. She has the gentlest soul. She follows me around and seems to be so happy just to be close. She likes to cozy up with me on the sofa and watch TV with me. She loves to go on rides in the car.

I broke a bone in my leg shortly after receiving Amelia, and she instinctively knew I couldn't walk fast anymore. She adjusted her gait to mine and constantly looked up at me to make sure I was all right. Being a German Shepherd, she takes her role of protector very seriously, yet is very gentle and affectionate.

As Amelia has aged, she has developed some nerve degeneration in her hindquarters. Through the generosity of AARF supporters, she is currently receiving physical therapy including acupuncture treatments and exercise on an underwater treadmill. She is very alert, her spirit is strong, and her level of mobility still allows her to enjoy life.

The first thing I see every morning is her sweet face looking into mine. I can't help but start the day off with a smile. Amelia came into my life when I needed her, and she needed me. Some things are meant to be.

 *Joyce Durdin*

Border Collie Dolly

We have always had a farm dog, and they have all been Border Collies. Despite the typical characteristics of this breed, none of ours have been true sheep dogs. They were farm dogs. Not even pets, really. They would greet visitors and family and serve as an effective deterrent to those who might not be welcome. They were always present and watchful at chore time. They kept coyotes away from the sheep pen, deer out of the garden, and occasionally salesmen in their vehicles. They played ball, kept the barn cats in line, and were protective of the family, especially the kids. All of our dogs through the years were valued members of the family and farm enterprise. And then there was Dolly.

We live on a small (very small) farm. Since my husband, Don, was a professional shepherd and I a fiber artist, we have always had sheep.

Our last dog, Hank, was killed in a freak accident two years ago. We both missed having a dog, and the howling coyotes at night made us nervous with new lambs on the ground. But neither of us was willing to take on another puppy, regardless of the cute factor. So we checked out the alternatives. Few farm-suitable breeds were available at the local animal shelters, and there were no Border Collies. So with some reservations, we filled out the paperwork and applied to the Nebraska Border Collie Rescue (NBCR).

Paperwork is putting it mildly. One of our references said they first thought we were adopting a foreign child. While the process was intimidating, we soon found the people were not. And we soon realized what the big fuss was about: making sure their adoptables go to appropriate homes. We are grateful for the work this rescue does.

We passed the home inspection and were invited to look over the selection of dogs waiting for adoption. We were impressed with the rescue's diligence in making sure to place the right dog with the *right* family, and we jumped at the chance to meet the first suggested candidate.

At the rescue we were told, "She's female aggressive." Looks of doubts were exchanged. The scramble of toenails on tile should have prepared us for the black-and-white bullet that shot into the room. The flying furball was uncontrollable, except for brief moments when a treat was cause for a pause, until she was finally reined in by a leash. She was nothing like the Border Collies we had known. Her ears were erect and her coat sleek and short. A smooth coat, we were told, who was likely a purebred. And what a deal: She even came in a crate.

We brought Doilidh (a.k.a. Dolly) home on Father's day. As predicted, she was a challenge. At 18 months old, after having been confined all her life and put through unknown stressful circumstances—not to mention being a Border Collie—she was energetic to say the least. She had a few behavioral problems, but it was clear she was highly intelligent and eager to please. She quickly learned some manners: no more jumping on people; sit for attention; come for treats.

As the adoption trial period was coming to an end, I asked Don if he thought we should keep her. He raised an eyebrow and replied, "Do you really want to do the last few weeks over with another one?"

I sent an email saying we were keeping her.

Six months later Dolly had effectively wagged, whined, and won her way into our hearts, and much to our kids' astonishment, into our house! For the first time in over 30 years, we had a semi-house dog. It was just practical; it was easier for me to let her in the house than to try to keep track of her, even with a fenced yard.

It wasn't long until Dolly was doing her best to fit in. If I was working in the shop, she picked up the scraps of wood. She was often underfoot, wanting to help. Of course, she was about as much help as a two-year-old, but she gradually learned to stay out of the way. While we picked apples, Dolly did too. When we cut and stacked wood for the winter, she would drag small limbs to make a pile of her own.

She has been with us for two years now. She lies at our feet while we eat supper and spends the evening beside Don's chair. She loves company of the human kind. She still hates other dogs.

Over the last year or so, Dolly has moved up in status and title. She is now living up to her heritage by becoming who she was always meant to be: a sheep dog. We knew she had potential, and now she is proving it. She lets us know when the sheep are sick, out, or otherwise up to no good. Her reaction to her first baby lamb was with the same delight as that of our two-legged small visitors. She tells Don when it's time to do chores or get the sheep in. She is not, and never will be a trial stock dog. But she does what she was meant to do, which is what we need her to do.

At precisely 2:45 p.m., Dolly watches for Don to come home from work and paces the floor if he's late. She knows which days I'm leaving for work by the clothes I'm wearing when I come downstairs.

Dolly knows to stay on the grass while we work in the garden. She alerts us to unwelcome guests in the yard and garden: deer, voles, snakes, and recently, a woodchuck in the shop. The rabbits and squirrels run for cover. Stalky the cat, who is 10+ years Dolly's senior, is tolerated. They occasionally meet in the house and exchange glances, but Dolly has learned to restrain herself with only an occasional "be nice" admonishment.

Sometime after she came to us, we pieced together some of Dolly's story, and we realized that she was actually at the shelter the very day we first went looking for a dog. But she wasn't ready for us. She needed to recover from a case of kennel cough before they turned her over to NBCR.

Occasionally things are just meant to be, and Dolly was meant to be with us. She wasn't exactly what we expected, or maybe even wanted. But she was what we needed. And we like to think she needed us and the things we could give her—a forever home, complete with sheep, and a job on a farm—everything a Border Collie was meant to have. Our farm is the place where she can be the dog she was meant to be. Yes, we'll definitely be keeping her.

 *Rhonda McClure*

Why Leave?

Growing up I had always been timid around most dogs, so naturally I never imagined that I would have my own. This all changed when I got married. My husband grew up with a dog and desperately wanted us to get one. With my husband's persistence, I finally gave in. He suggested we get a Bulldog or a Boston Terrier. I quickly decided against the Bulldog due to their size and penchant for slobbering, so we went with the Boston Terrier. It was one of the best decisions I had ever made. The newest addition to our family soon became a sweet little girl we named Munjoy.

Munjoy was bored while we were at work, so we began thinking about getting a second dog. We looked at many adoptable Boston Terriers on Petfinder.com, and I responded similarly to each one my husband showed me: "Cute, but not for us." Deep down I was unsure if I was ready to care for another dog. The more I thought about it, the more I didn't think adding another Boston was going to work out.

That was until I saw one particular dog. The ad said simply, "Vinny in ME" (meaning Maine), and much to my surprise, I instantly fell for him. I couldn't stop staring at his picture; he looked like the happiest dog I had ever seen, despite the fact that he had spent all his days in a puppy mill. Looking at the love in his face made me forget about all the doubts and fears I had about getting another dog. At that moment, I knew I had to meet him.

My husband filled out an application, and within a few days Vinny stopped by for a visit. Munjoy and I waited outside our building until the handsome black-and-white Boston came walking down the sidewalk. My heart nearly jumped out of my chest; I just wanted to run up and squeeze him.

Vinny seemed anxious as he approached. When we headed inside, Vinny charged up the front steps and without stopping ran straight into the door, causing him to flop back down the steps. Luckily Vinny had an easier time once we were inside. He was intrigued by the new scents and sounds, and Munjoy was very interested in him. Vinny eventually tired himself out and decided to take a nap in Munjoy's bed, which was about two sizes too small. My thoughts were running wild, and I began making a mental list of all the things I would need to get for Vinny. The first item on the list was definitely a bigger bed.

Saying goodbye to Vinny that evening was extremely difficult for me, as I wanted Vinny and I wanted him now. A few long days later we heard from Vinny's foster parents—Vinny was ours!

The next few months were emotionally and physically draining. Vinny was timid and anxious, and some days he refused to eat from his bowl, at which point I had to get down on the floor with him and feed him by hand, one kibble at a time. The struggle didn't end there. Vinny was uncomfortable doing his business and would hold it for what seemed like forever. On the most difficult days, we would walk around for nearly two hours before going back inside defeated. But with patience and encouragement, Vinny eventually mastered eating from the bowl and doing his duty outside. With each passing day, Vinny became more confident and even began snuggling and playing with Munjoy.

Vinny had made great progress with us, but little did I know Vinny would soon be put to the test. We had been told by Vinny's foster parents that according to his previous foster, he would attempt to run away if given the chance. One afternoon, about a year after we adopted him, Vinny, Munjoy, and I went down to the basement of our condo to put some boxes in storage. I didn't have them on their leashes, as we were inside the building, and I had no idea that someone had left the side door open. Munjoy and Vinny bolted outside. I dropped the boxes and immediately ran out after them. Luckily Munjoy, being a fairly well-trained dog, stopped when she heard me calling, and with a guilty look on her face she came back to me. To my disbelief, Vinny, who had no training and could barely sit on command, had decided that instead of exploring the world he should sit on the front steps and wait for me. Vinny had found his forever home, and he was not going to leave.

To this day Vinny continues to teach, love, and surprise us.

 *Jamie Becksvoort*

Doggie Doings

Dangerous Dinner: Daisy May and Scooter Pie were surrendered to the humane society together. I did not need two dogs, but they needed me, so I let my heartstrings win out to my reason and adopted them both. Scooter came home that day, and Daisy May came a few days later after her spay. It quickly became apparent that Daisy was sick, so I took her to the vet. X-rays showed nothing wrong, but exploratory surgery revealed that she had ingested some sort of cloth, and its threads were acting like a garrote. The humane society had no way of knowing that "no time for the dog" was code for "we let her eat something that would cause a slow and painful death from obstructed bowels" when her owners surrendered her. The vet removed 12 inches of her bowels, and Daisy now thrives. She's definitely an odd little dog, and it turns out that she and her "brother" want nothing to do with each other. No matter, there are plenty of other things to keep a dog occupied in our home, like foster puppies! -*Andrea Newborg*

Short Legs, Tall Order: Since my husband has been diagnosed with a seizure disorder, Napolean has stayed by his side. One day, when I arrived home from work, I could tell before entering the house that my husband had a seizure because Napolean was sounding his alarm—a distressful sounding bark. Although my husband has always been a cat person (we have six cats), he has become very close to this Dachshund, who keeps him company during the day, even giving him rides on his motorized wheelchair. I believe that God had a plan for Napolean to come into our lives, and I treasure our mini long-haired boy. -*Elaine N. Robinson*

Boxer Blues

Memphis came into rescue from a local shelter after being picked up on the street as stray. This poor boy's front leg had been severely fractured to the point that it was twisted and had healed that way. Memphis was unable to walk normally on all four legs and was forced to walk on the outside of his front pad; stretching his front tendons and bone. The Boxer rescue that took him in set up an appointment with a surgeon to see if there was anything that could be done to help straighten out his leg. After examining Memphis, the surgeon contacted the rescue and told them there was a surgery they could do to help give Memphis the quality of life he deserved.

I had just gone through the adoption application process and was waiting to hear back from the rescue on which dog might be the right fit for us. We had picked out two or three dogs from the adoption website that we thought would be perfect for us, and Memphis was not one of them.

One day we received an unforgettable email from the director of the rescue. We were on vacation at the time, emailing back and forth with the director, who suggested that Memphis would be a good match for us. At first I wasn't sure. I had just gone through several years of surgeries (one being a plated leg break) and numerous other issues with my other dog: cancer, congestive heart failure, etc., which is why I had dismissed the thought of having to take care of a dog needing a major surgery. Due to diminished quality of life, I had just sent my other dog to the Rainbow Bridge three months prior to reaching out to this rescue, and that loss left a huge hole in my heart.

I emailed the rescue and told them I was not sure about Memphis and explained why. I can recall their words exactly. "Well, if you don't want him, we can continue to look." It was said so nicely, yet those words made me realize that this was not about me, it was about him: Memphis. I emailed the rescue back in tears and said I would love to take him. I wanted to be sure we could take him prior to his surgery and that he could recover in his forever home.

During the two weeks in which we had Memphis before his surgery, the two of us did not hit it off. He immediately bonded with my boyfriend but would not come to me or acknowledge me. To be fair, I didn't want much to do with him, either, thinking he had issues. Then my boyfriend took a trip, leaving Memphis and me home alone together. The first few days I just went through the motions, taking Memphis out and feeding him. He kept his distance from me those first few days, too.

I remember sitting on the couch one evening while Memphis was across the room, lying on his bed and just staring at me. At this point he had never come to me for affection. I started crying uncontrollably, thinking to myself, what I have done? Did I adopt this dog too soon?

I was crying for my Sam who had just passed, until suddenly I felt a heavy head on my knee. As I turned to look down, it was Memphis, sitting at my feet and staring up at me, as if to say, "It's okay, I'm here for you."

I bent down to really pet and touch him for the first time. He responded by kissing me and laying his head on my lap with a large sigh. Right then I realized that *I* was the one with the issues, not Memphis. Memphis came to me in a time I needed him most, and from that day on, he holds a very special place in my heart.

At the end of the second week, we received a call that his surgery had been scheduled. A specialist assisted in the rebuilding of his leg, which had to be re-broken and two inches of bone growth had to be removed. They literally patched his leg backed together and pinned it for six months, during which time he continuously suffered bad infections. Memphis was heavily medicated with antibiotics and pain pills for most of the time.

I had never seen such a brave and special boy as Memphis. He kept his Boxer spirit throughout the whole process and allowed us to care for his wounds with no complaints. Not only has he taught us the joy of life with a Boxer, but he has filled a hole in my heart that I thought could never heal.

I have had Memphis for three years now, and he has brought piles of love into my life. I'll be forever grateful to the rescue for matching him with us. It has been two years since the surgery, and I still cry every time I see Memphis run because he could never do that before. Although he will never be an athlete, his quality of life has changed dramatically, as has the quality of mine. Memphis (the city) may be known for the blues, but there is nothing "bluesy" about our Memphis. He is one big, happy bundle of joy!

 *Kelly Taylor*

A Spoonful of...Vaseline

We took our granddaughter to the Defiance County (Ohio) Humane Society to look for a Dalmatian, but instead we found a Cocker Spaniel.

He was roaming the city streets and had been at the Humane Society, unnamed, for four months. After being adopted out once, he was returned the next morning for growling at their children. Fortunately, this is a no-kill shelter.

He was a buff-and-white Cocker Spaniel with very droopy eyes. His long tail was unusual, as most Cockers' tails are docked, and it went around in circles when he was happy. Most people called him "the dog with the tail."

Even though we didn't take him home that first day, we couldn't get those big, sad eyes out of our minds. We saw his photo in an adoption ad in the local newspaper, which compelled us to stop by the shelter again to see him. My husband really wanted to adopt him even though we already had two Cockers. I finally told him to do whatever he wanted. The next day when I got home from work, I looked out the window and did a double take. There he was tied to the clothesline pole. We decided to name him Barkley.

He was very polite and well-behaved—the only Cocker we ever had who did not try to take over our bed, preferring instead his own pillow on the floor. Barkley knew how to roll over and how to stand up on his hind legs to beg, and he also "danced" on his hind legs, turning around in circles.

We are members of a walking club and do a six-mile walk almost every weekend. Barkley usually went with us. Sometimes we would walk twelve miles in one day, and Barkley didn't mind. When we went away for a weekend of walking, Barkley came too. He walked with us in Indiana, Michigan, and Illinois.

Barkley had arthritis, which gradually slowed him down and caused him to walk with a limp. One day Barkley could not finish a walk and needed to be carried for the last three blocks. That was no easy feat, as Barkley was very lanky and heavy (41 pounds). He was rather large for a Cocker Spaniel, with long legs and very big paws.

Barkley always had a bad habit of eating things he shouldn't. He ate seashells, stones, and bark chips. He ate a beaded craft project. He also ate a suction cup and a plastic bottle cap, but there was worse to come.

One day we returned from vacation and picked the dogs up at the kennel. Barkley was very lethargic, but we thought he was just tired from all the excitement at the kennel. He didn't want to eat, which was extremely unusual for him. We could only get him to eat soft food in small amounts. Since he had most of his teeth removed and the rest were bad, we thought he just couldn't chew the dry food anymore. We were not too concerned.

The following week he ate less every day, so we took Barkley to the vet, who did some blood tests. He thought the arthritis medication was causing a stomach problem, so he swapped that medication for two new ones. That afternoon Barkley vomited a three-inch long splinter of wood. He fell down on the floor and just laid there for a few minutes. I called the vet's office and was told to make Barkley eat some Vaseline in case there were more splinters inside of him. Getting a dog to eat Vaseline is no easy task, especially when the dog is sick and grumpy.

When we got the test results back, Barkley's red blood count was half of what it should have been, his white blood count was elevated, and his protein level was low. The vet told us that Barkley was in "serious trouble." That was his polite way of telling us that Barkley might not survive the weekend. But by Sunday, Barkley was acting a little better and wanting to eat people food.

Barkley had more checkups and more blood tests. He was starting to hate going to the vet's office, so he refused to walk, and I had to carry him to the exam room. He lost a total of seven pounds before he was once again eating his food and all the treats he could get. That little splinter of wood ended up costing us hundreds of dollars and nearly cost Barkley his life.

As time passed, Barkley was able to take a few very short walks with us, but his idea of a walk became checking out the fire hydrant in our front yard to see which other dogs had visited that day. After sniffing the area, Barkley was ready to go back to his pillow. Even though he wasn't very active, his tail always wagged when he saw us, and he greeted me at the door every day when I get home from work.

 *Becky Corwin-Adams*

Big on Beagles

My wife and I acquired our first Beagle about nine months after we were married, and we always named them after Peter Pan characters. Peter (the Beagle) was my boy, my son (as we had no kids), and the center of our universe: a beautiful tri-colored Beagle with red and blue ticks all over his white parts. After five years we decided to get him a mate and acquired Wendy from a hunting buddy, who gave her to us as a present. Peter and Wendy were an inseparable mated pair for the next 12 years.

Later in life Peter lost his sight and hearing and slept most of his days away. Wendy was battling a mass in her stomach, which seemed benign, and other than its weight, it didn't seem to bother her. That year on my wife's birthday, a routine vet visit revealed that Peter's kidneys had failed, and he should be put down. We had him on IVs for days—we didn't want to have my wife's birthday be the day we lost my first "son," and saying goodbye was very hard. The day I put him down was the worst day of my life. Two months later, the tumor in Wendy's stomach became cancerous. All her pining for her mate had slowed her down, and she gave up. She had to be put down, too. I had lost both my children.

During the two months after Peter's departure, I had started adoption proceedings for Sasha in hopes that another Beagle would help Wendy. Unfortunately, Beagle Rescue of Southern Maryland's (BRSM) screening process took time. Against a lot of well-wishers' advice, we adopted Sasha only weeks after Wendy died.

It's a good thing I didn't listen to those well-wishers. The day I met Sasha, now Slightly, she jumped into my arms and snuggled into my neck, as if I had been her owner all along. Being 15 years younger than both Peter and Wendy, she was a complete handful and what sadness I had from the loss of my first two Beagles was filled with oopsies, Beagle bolts, long trail walks, snuggling on the couch, and pure happiness. Because of Sasha, I got back into running and currently am training for marathons!

If it weren't for BSRM, I think my wife and I would have had a full meltdown. We had always had Beagles on the couch, in the yard, and in the big dog bed.

After Sasha we took in an old guy who could not be adopted, "Tootles," and a year after him we took in a young Beagle for Slightly named Roscoe, whom we gave the Lost Boy name Nibs. The young Beagles wake me up for running and keep me motivated, and no amount of messes or problems bring me down. Tootles, the old guy, is on borrowed time (we estimate his age at 13-18), and with all his ailments we assumed he would have been with us only eight or nine months. Now he has been with us over two years! Tootles was an old, worn-out hunting dog someone abandoned. BRSM found him in very poor shape and nursed him back to health. He had been with them almost three years when we decided to give him a home. He takes the most effort, with four or five meds twice a day and all the problems that an old dog can have, but it's all worth it when he picks up a scent for a rabbit on our walks. He perks up and you would think he is four or five, not the old guy he is supposed to be.

I will always have Beagles, and when there is a vacancy, I will give BRSM a call and get another (maybe two)!

 *Justyn Cox*

Rocky and Adrienne

I have been fortunate to be loved by dogs for most of my 70 years. I've got many "tails" to tell! Today, I'll focus on Rocky, the dog I believe God sent me specifically, knowing what was to come.

When I met Rocky, Boomer, a Rottie, and Amber, a Weimaraner, were happily living with my husband and me. It was springtime, and all of a sudden Amber flew downstairs and out the back door, barking her head off! I couldn't imagine what would cause her to act like that and had to see what was happening outside. Lo and behold, the most adorable Pit-mix puppy was on the other side of the fence, clearly wanting to be friends with Boomer. His little tail was wagging and he looked so sweet and friendly.

The puppy walked toward the part of the fence where it meets our house, but my two dogs didn't pay attention to him there, so he went around to the third side of the fence to wag his butt and tail. I became concerned when I realized he wasn't wearing a collar, and no one was out looking for him. I live on Main Street of a busy city. I went out the gate and down the driveway with a leash in my hand to attempt to capture the little dickens and get him into a safe area. When he saw me, a BIG person, he got a bit nervous and backed up. I attempted bribery with doggie cookies, which didn't work, so I ended up hooking the leash and lassoing him. AHA!

It turned out this four-month-old wasn't going anyplace he didn't want to go. He planted his feet on the sidewalk and backed away, slipping out of the looped "collar." By this time I was out of breath due to a lung problem, so I said, "Okay, you, that's it!" I turned around and walked back up to the gate. I noticed he followed me and entered the yard with no problem, and he has followed me every step from that moment on.

I thought for sure someone would be looking for him, for he was truly precious, but for three days there was nothing in the papers and no one calling for a dog. By this time I thought, "Well, I'll just call him Rocky because it just goes with my name, Adrienne."

Three days later I overheard a group of kids talking as they walked by. Someone said, "Hey, doesn't that look like your dog?"

I came out and asked if they had a dog missing and for how long. The one boy said he lived three houses away on the other side of the street and had been missing his dog for three days. I told him to go home and get his leash, and I'd let him borrow my collar. About a half hour later, one of the older kids came back and said that the boy's mother didn't want the dog. Did I want him?

Didn't want the dog? I couldn't imagine that, as I had completely fallen in love with him. Of course, I said yes!

Boomer taught Rocky good manners throughout the summer, but in early August, Boomer died suddenly. Then, three weeks later, Amber died following surgery. If I had been left with no dogs, I would have been beyond bereft. That's why I truly believe God sent me Rocky out of the blue.

 *Adrienne*

Losing a Friend

B eetle Bailey passed away last Saturday. She had been battling seizures for the past several weeks. During that time, I spoon-fed her and carried her outside to do her duties. We visited the vet a lot during those seven weeks, and as usual, Bailey fought back again and again.

We adopted this "young" lady about two years ago. She was nine years old, skinny at 42 pounds, and unspayed. She had lost her sight from diabetes and had several tumors that needed to be removed. When her owner realized he wouldn't be able to care for her, he surrendered her to Golden Retriever rescue.

Bailey battled chronic ear problems, hyperparathyroidism (the excessive production of the parathyroid hormone), four different type bladder infections, one after another, and finally getting her diabetes glucose curve under control. We'd had many ups and downs, but through it all Bailey, had been a trooper.

The rescue gave her eye surgery, which restored her sight. They helped her manage her diabetes, had her spayed, and had those nasty tumors removed. During her spay, the vet found even more tumors in addition to the ones below and around her shoulders.

Bailey had a zest for life. Even when we thought it was time a few weeks ago, she surprised us once again. Leaving the vet, we placed her in the back of the SUV (she hadn't walked in weeks). As my wife, Carrie, and I drove into our driveway, we stopped and paused for a few minutes; there was Beetle, standing up between the front seats and looking at us.

Many friends told me that Beetle was in love with me. Even Carrie mentioned it many times. I will never forget Beetle Bailey, the Golden who danced and sang for her breakfast and supper; the Golden who demanded belly rubs and insisted I rub her nose; the Golden who surprised us again and again.

We never lost sight that we wanted to make sure Bailey had a good quality of life. You know, she was my friend, my Golden, and my sweetheart.

The TV room is now empty; the house is quiet. The barks that once echoed throughout our home are sadly missing. The cats and our other two Goldens are wondering where their Beetle has gone. We have lost a beautiful friend whom we miss dearly.

 *Greg and Carrie Korycki*

Oh, How Things Change

It was Thanksgiving weekend, and my stepson was in the back yard. He was throwing pebbles at the kitchen window to get my attention. When I looked outside, I saw him standing there with a puppy! I could see that the puppy was very skinny and obviously had been on its own for quite some time. I called to my husband, and we both went outside.

The puppy was a mixture of excited and scared. I could tell he wanted to run up to us but was unsure of our response. Not having any dog food, I fixed him a plate of leftover turkey and vegetables. He came to me for that and ate the entire plate in a matter of seconds. He was so hungry.

All around us are people in other neighborhoods who let their dogs run loose. The unrestrained dogs frequently come into our neighborhood looking for garbage cans and handouts. We assumed that this puppy belonged to someone like that, so we left him outside and went back in the house.

Later that day, when my husband went out front to put up Christmas lights and decorations, he found the puppy still hanging around our yard. The puppy stayed with my husband the whole time he was working outside, and when night came, he lay down on our back porch. Living in the South, the days are fairly comfortable, but the nights can be cold. That night the temperature was suppose to dip down into the 20's, so I found an old comforter and put it on the back porch for the dog.

Monday morning the puppy was still hanging around, so my husband bought a small bag of dog food. Our intention was to ask around to find out if anyone knew anything about the puppy. If we were unsuccessful in locating the owner, we would take him to the SPCA. We both had always agreed that we didn't want a dog because of the time, expense, and mess that came with dog ownership.

And the puppy did create quite a mess in our back yard. By Thursday he had chewed plants, flowers, a bucket, and the air conditioner line. He had dug into all the flower beds and spread black mulch all over the yard.

But I was hopelessly in love with him. So when my husband came to me that morning asking what I intended to do about the puppy, my eyes filled up with tears. I declared that I wanted to keep him and that his name was Tyler.

I took him to the vet on Saturday and found out that he was approximately six months old and in good health. He weighed 26 pounds and was estimated to reach a maximum weight of 50 pounds.

I thought that was a perfect-sized dog.

When the temperatures at night fell into the teens, we borrowed a cage and let him sleep in our bedroom. My husband and I agreed that he would have to live outside, but as time went on, Tyler began sleeping inside every night, until eventually his time inside was extended longer and longer each morning.

Now Tyler lives in the house. The cage was replaced with big, soft pillows for Tyler to sleep on in the bedroom and the living room. He loves people, other dogs, and especially kids. He loves to ride in the car and take long walks. I take him everywhere with me. He is much loved. Turns out that he isn't too expensive, and the time spent on him is a joy. But... he *is* still messy.

 *Suzanne Gill*

Duck Brings Comfort

The beautiful little puppy was just six days old when he lost his mother. He came into our rescue with all the trappings and fears characteristic of puppy mill dogs. The rescue volunteers lovingly bottle fed him, and the vets helped him through his health issues, but everything he had missed in his early days of life left him a very phobic puppy. He was terrified of wind, thunder, sudden noises, certain lights, the swimming pool, many people, and life in general.

He joined our family, and we named him Gus. We were determined to provide him all the love, security, and confidence he needed to enjoy life. But in spite of all our love, Gus still needed something else to comfort him in times of stress. He found it in a big, yellow stuffed duck, which he chose out of the toy box. It soon became his substitute mom, endearingly named Duck.

When tired or frightened, Gus would cuddle up with Duck, drawing it near him with his paws, kneading its soft body, and sucking its bill much like he was nursing. When Duck required mending or washing, Gus supervised and patiently waited its return.

When we adopted Joy, another rescue puppy needing special love and attention, Gus fell in love with her. They had two weeks of playtime and bonding prior to Joy's surgery to remove her damaged foot and leg. During her first post-surgical night home, Gus sat in front of her open crate door with a furrowed brow, watching her every movement. After a short while, he quietly left the bedroom. He returned to crawl carefully into her crate to offer his restless little sister the gift from his heart: his tattered yellow Duck.

 *Kas Mantz*

Doggie Doings

Walk It Off: I adopted Fred, a Bloodhound, from an individual who kept him in horrible living conditions. Overcoming his physical issues was challenging, but most difficult was his fierce dog aggression. I researched and hired trainers and saw little improvement, but I wasn't giving up. Ultimately I solved most of Fred's behavioral issues by walking him until he was drained of energy. In turn, this helped me get into shape. We walked so much that recently he was featured in Austin Fit Magazine as one of Austin's Fittest Dogs. Fred has taken more work than any dog I have ever known, but he has given me back more than I could ask for. He continues to surprise and impress me as time goes by. *-Kari Terrell*

Making Connections: Pebbles was in Indiana; I was in Texas, but I felt an unexplained draw to adopt her. Once approved, I booked a flight and was on my way to get her. When the big day came, I flew to Chicago, rented a car, and drove for about two hours. One moment it was midnight; the next it was 1 a.m.! It turns out I had passed by South Bend and lost an hour. I pressed on. At 2 a.m. I checked into a hotel for a restless night. By 9 a.m. I had Pebbles in my arms, and we were soon back on our way back to Texas. Pebbles was a hit at the airport; everyone we met was touched by my efforts to bring her "home." She even got to meet the captain of our aircraft! I finally understood the strong connection: Pebbles' home was meant to be with me. *-Erika Pinkoczi*

Lucky Dog

Hello everybody! I want to tell you my rescue tale, and I'll let you know ahead of time it has a very happy ending.

I'm a handsome mixed-breed dog of German Shorthair Pointer and cattle dog lineage. My birth name is Freckles, probably because I look like I have a million black freckles all over me. I was nine months old when my dad lost his job. He became really depressed and realized I would be better off in a new home.

Within a week I was in my foster home, walking, playing, and snuggling. But I had a hard time sharing the spotlight with the other foster dogs. Sometimes I'd get angry and snap at my foster brother. I really longed to be an only dog where I could have all the attention to myself.

After six weeks I felt more relaxed and had learned to sit, stay, come, and walk pretty well on a leash, so my foster parents decided it was time to start searching for my forever home. Quickly, a young couple found me. They had just bought their first house and had two cats. Did I mention that I like cats? They wanted a jogging companion and a dog to take to work sometimes.

While we waited for the approval process to be completed, they took me for a weekend trial. We went to their family farm, and I showed them how I could run without a leash but not run away. I thoroughly impressed the grandparents. I even got to spend the night with the couple. I met their cats, who seemed to think I was boring, but that's just how cats are, right?

When my new parents came to pick me up for good, my foster parents cried, but they said it was because they were so happy that I had found the perfect home. We packed up my bones, blankets, dog bed, and leash, and I said goodbye. I was going to miss them, but I just couldn't pass up the opportunity to be top dog!

After a year at my forever home, my new mom decided to give my old foster family an update. We met at a park nearby. When I saw my foster parents, I immediately showed them how much I had grown up by walking without a leash next to my new mom and dad. I even showed them that I can come when they call me by my new distinguished name, Cooper. My foster family was thrilled to see how happy I am. I am a lucky dog, and I know that.

I believe there is a family out there for every dog. I mean, look at me; I got exactly what I wanted, which was to be the much-loved only dog. I'm thankful for my foster family and for Dogs Deserve Better rescue, especially because they were all willing to let me stay for a while until the perfect forever home was found.

 Cooper, Translated by Sarah Guenther

Polishing Penny

We've had Penny for four years now and can't imagine life without her. She is definitely my husband's dog, even though it was me who found her at the Buffalo SPCA; she is madly in love with him. That's okay—my boys love me.

The shelter had named her Penny, so we kept it and just added the middle name Ann. Don't laugh, but that's my sister's middle name, and since I never had a daughter to name after her, Penny is her Goddog instead of Goddaughter. Anyway, after our first dog, Bosch, died at age 13, we swore we would wait a while to adopt a playmate for our other dog,

Bart. We thought it would be nice to just have Bart and spoil him. Well, that didn't last long because I kept looking at the SPCA website, and one day there she was. I was hooked.

Penny is all white with one black ear and a black circle around one eye. She looks like two completely different dogs depending on how you look at her. She has curly, wavy fur with a few black spots on her back. They actually had her listed as an English Springer Spaniel/Dalmatian mix.

I was very excited to take Penny for a walk when I went to the SPCA that Friday afternoon. She was only 23 pounds, and I could see all her ribs. She had a flea infestation and was starving. They had spayed her, but what I didn't realize at the time is that she must have been in a lot of pain; her incision was red and not healing. From the first glance she gave me, I was hooked. Penny was so lovable and affectionate, even though she had been severely mistreated.

I put my name down to hold her for us and came back the next day with Bart and my husband, Ron, but when we went to her kennel, she was nowhere to be found. My heart sank! We finally found out that she was in the back in the doggie hospital because she was very ill, wouldn't eat, and had the runs. She was just plain miserable. They let Ron see her, and he gave his okay to adopt her, but we decided we'd wait until she was well. We made lots of calls during the next week to check on her every day, and I think they were surprised that we still wanted her. But we did!

Finally, the next Saturday Penny was released to go home. She was loving, liked Bart, and instantly formed a strong bond with Ron. She ran right up to him and sat on his lap the whole first day. We thought her passiveness was just because she was a calm dog, but we were soon to find out she was still very sick.

A day or two later we took her for her complimentary vet visit, only to find out very bad news. The vet took one look at her gums and skin and said she had problems—dog gums should be pink, not white. She took blood work and said she'd call with results. About an hour later we got the call: Penny had a very serious blood infection from all the flea bites. She was actually...dying! If she didn't have a blood transfusion within the next day, it would be over.

Our vet told us that we could, of course, take her back to the SPCA and either get our money back or get another dog, but we knew Penny would be put down because they couldn't afford to give her what she needed. My head was spinning; we only had her for three days, and we already loved her, but we couldn't help but wonder about the cost and outcome of her medical care.

My husband said to call the emergency clinic and find out what was involved. They told us that if she only needed one transfusion, it would be about $750. We decided to give her a chance at life, so we rushed her over, and they gave her the transfusion that night. The doctor said we didn't want to hear from them—no news would be good news—and to call back around 10 p.m. We could hardly wait to call, and when we did, we got good news. The transfusion went well, and Penny only needed one. The pink was coming back to her skin already.

Surprisingly there was one problem that became apparent the next morning. When Penny felt better, she became very aggressive with her food as a result of being starved. We had to deal with that for a long time by feeding separately.

Penny's journey back to normal was a long path. She had to have special food, and even though she was always hungry, it had to be in small quantities, or she would throw it up. It took a couple of months to get her into a normal routine. Slowly her ribs started fading away, and you won't believe this: Now we have to have her on low fat food! She is a joy and we know we made the right decision to give her a chance at life. She still has her older brother, Bart, who is now 16½. I have found her defending him from her new brother, Jackson, who wants to constantly play and roughhouse.

Everyone who meets Penny loves her because she cuddles up to them and makes each person feel like she loves them, too. I think maybe someday she would be a good candidate to go visit nursing homes, as I'm sure she could spread a lot of joy.

 *Sue Kasprzyk*

Polo's First Night

This is the timeline of Polo's first night in foster care after being picked up from his transport to Colorado:

9:00 p.m. Polo arrives at his new foster home, has a quick walk around the front yard and down the block, explores the house, and meets his new foster siblings.

9:05 p.m. Polo's new human foster sister cleans and treats his ears; they are smelly and squishy and infected.

9:15 p.m. Polo explores the back yard with foster siblings.

9:30 p.m. Polo eats two cups of food in 30 seconds flat.

9:35 p.m. Polo unrolls the TP in the bathroom.

9:45 p.m. Polo gets snapped at for the first time by Ruby Roo, his Nova Scotia Duck Tolling Retriever foster sister, for trying to get on the bed.

10 p.m. Polo starts eating the laundry basket.

10 p.m.–11 p.m. Foster mom hangs out on the floor with Polo.

11 p.m. Foster mom crawls into bed, and Polo starts eating the laundry basket again, using the vacuum cleaner cord as floss.

11 p.m.–1 a.m. Foster mom and foster dad take turns trying to make Polo comfortable.

1 a.m.–2 a.m. Quiet... Or so we think.

2 a.m. Wake up to sound of running water—actually pee (he's already been out at least four times since 10 p.m.).

2:15 a.m. Foster mom finally decides maybe crating him for the night would work.

2:30 a.m. Crating does *not* work.

3 a.m. Polo finally gets situated on the bed with his smelly ears in his foster mom's face.

4:15 a.m. Foster dad's alarm goes off. Foster mom wants to hurt something/anything.

4:20 a.m. Polo can't decide whether to follow foster dad into the shower or paw foster mom's face until it is bleeding.

4:45 a.m. Polo finally snuggles in and all is well, until...

5:15 a.m. ...foster dad leaves for work, and Polo cries.

5:30 a.m. Polo snuggles back in with foster mom.

5:45 a.m. Alarm goes off, and Polo is AWAKE.

6:30 a.m. Polo eats another two cups of food in 30 seconds or less.

Is Polo a bad dog? Are we regretting fostering? Well, poor Charles, the bleary-eyed Beagle may disagree, as Beagles need their beauty sleep, but we don't regret it for a moment. This was just a typical first night in a foster home for a very good dog who just needs to learn some manners and gain confidence. Before we know it, Polo will be off to his new home, and we'll be in for another long night with a new foster dog.

 *Melanie Stelter*

Crate-Me-Not

Mandy actually rescued me. I was coming toward the end of a rough period in my life filled with losing a job I loved, depression, and self-hate. We found each other the weekend before I was going to start a new job that I stayed at for almost 10 years.

One of my brothers has 80 acres in a remote part of Arizona, and when I was visiting him that weekend, I also had a visit from a six-week-old puppy who someone had abandoned in the desert. While I was admiring how cute she was, I wondered how someone could be so evil to just dump a helpless little puppy in the middle of nowhere.

I wasn't really planning on getting a puppy because I was going to start a new job the following Monday, and I felt stressed as it was. But after playing with her for a while, I, of course, fell in love. I couldn't bear the thought of her not having a home because she already seemed to have had a rough beginning.

Mandy is a Border Collie-mix, all black with a black-and-white spotted stomach. Now that she is older, she has also grown some white fur on her paws, face, and rear end.

I talked to Mandy constantly on the hour drive back to my house. I told her everything would be okay, and she will come and live with me now. I named her Mandy because *White Christmas* is one of my favorite movies, and "Mandy" is my favorite song from that movie.

I felt bad when Mandy was a puppy because she was my only dog, and I had to leave her home alone while I was at work. After reading about puppies, I decided to crate train her for her own safety. I didn't want her to chew on an electrical cord and get shocked because I wasn't there to watch her.

Mandy got used to being in the crate while I was away, and I felt good about her being in it because I knew she was safe. Luckily I was close enough to work that I went home at lunch every day and let her out to play for my lunch hour.

As Mandy grew older and got bigger, she started becoming upset when I crated her, jumping up and down, whining, and crying. That broke my heart, but I kept crating her because I knew it was the safest place for her.

Six or seven months later I installed a doggie door and decided she was old enough to not be in the crate while I was gone. Maybe I should have waited longer because that's when she started destroying my house. Even though she had plenty of toys and rawhide bones, Mandy tore up my carpet. I got new carpet, and she tore it up again. She tore up my mattress, chewed on the coffee table, chewed on the wood deck in the back yard, and tore up two couches.

When I asked her veterinarian why she was so destructive, he said that she was lonely and always looking for me; when she found my scent, she dug trying to find me. Wow—that made me feel horrible for leaving her alone.

Mandy hates loud noises, and I think it's because the weekend I found her there was a big storm by my brother's house. It was strong enough to rip down his airplane hangar and twist the metal. Whenever we have a thunderstorm, Mandy hides in the bathtub. I always bring her a toy and tell her she's a good girl because I want her to feel secure.

Despite everything I went through when Mandy was a puppy, I never realized how capable I was to love another living creature with all my heart. She was so good for me because she taught me how to love unconditionally and how to exercise patience. She taught me to be considerate and unselfish because I had to make sure she was taken care of, too. She showed me respect and appreciation for the little things in life through her enjoyment of simply taking a long walk, getting brushed, or playing with toys for hours.

Mandy and I have been together for more than 10 years now, and I can't imagine a better dog in my life. We found each other at the perfect time, which reaffirms to me how things are sometimes meant to be.

 *Mary Schaut*

Behind the Cute

Little Carla was rescued from a puppy mill, where she had been born and kept for breeding. She was saved by Rescue a Golden of Arizona (RAG) when she was between three and five years old. She struggled to overcome the experience of living in a cage in a barn her whole life.

When Carla arrived, she had been shaved bald because of tick and flea infestations in her skin. She had several kinds of worms and kennel cough. RAG boarded her with a veterinarian, who gave her inoculations, spayed her, and cared for her before I took her as a foster dog. I called her Little Carla because she never weighed more than 48 pounds, which is small for a Golden.

Carla had never been in a house, nor had she been socialized. She was fearful of the outdoors, having never experienced running free in a back yard or going for a walk. She was frightened and wouldn't make eye contact. In fact, the only place she felt safe was in a crate. For two weeks, I sat on a mattress in the kitchen every evening with my two other Goldens and watched TV. Every night Little Carla would crawl a bit closer, until finally one night she inched up into my lap, put her forehead to my forehead, and looked into my eyes. It was the first time she had made eye contact with me.

As Carla became more socialized, and her beautiful mahogany coat grew back, she began welcoming people who came to visit our home. Nevertheless, the outdoor world remained a frightening place. Outside she would turn away from strangers, as if she believed by not looking at them they didn't exist.

Of course, I adopted Carla. Her way of demanding attention was to lick my hand or leg or just come put her head on my lap. My older Golden, Sunny, became Carla's surrogate mother, licking her and sleeping close to her. Carla never learned to play with the other dogs but was content to watch the action.

Carla was normally very healthy, so when she started drinking large amounts of water and urinating frequently, I suspected diabetes. An ultrasound showed she had malignant tumors of the liver and spleen, which were inoperable but not painful. I was told that one of them would eventually rupture, and she was given three months to live.

Fortunately, Carla survived comfortably for over a year before we had to say goodbye. She was cremated with her favorite toy, a yellow stuffed duck that she carried around and slept with. Her ashes are scattered in the only outdoor place she finally felt safe—our back yard. Carla was with us for over four years.

Anyone who buys a dog from a pet store should know what breeding dogs in puppy mills must suffer to produce those adorable little fur balls who are put on display for sale. Despite the denials of the pet store personnel, this is almost always the case.

 *Ruth A. Steffes*

Gummy and Sweet

I stood outside a gas station in the rain waiting for a transport. Several rescues where getting dogs from a kill shelter. I was there to meet the transport to pick up the small breed dogs. We open the van and there were over 50 dogs saved, but only 12 were to come with me. After I loaded my van and waited to get the transfer papers, I decided to look in on the other dogs and give them water for the hour drive they had until their next stop.

I glanced in and saw this little thing in a kennel with two Lab puppies. I pulled her out and noticed she was a little old long-hair Chihuahua who somehow got mixed in. The transport lady looked for her papers, but none were to be found. I told her I'd take her with me; because no one had papers on her, it seemed like fate had stepped in.

The next day I got a better look at her. She had to be more than 12 years old, and she only had one tooth left in her little mouth. I called the shelter from which she came, and they had no record of her, no answer for why she was on the transport.

This dog sat at our rescue for a few days, shy and timid— she never barked. One day I decided to take her home for the weekend. I took her to my mother's, and it was like they were meant for each other. Momma named her Taffy because she had no teeth and was "gummy and sweet." In return, Taffy gave Momma tons of kisses.

Taffy wouldn't follow me, but when my mother went in the house, Taffy sat at the door looking for her. My mom, of all people, offered to foster her, and Taffy followed her everywhere, sitting in my mom's lap or next to her no matter where she was, even at the piano.

Three months went by, and we still never heard Taffy bark. We thought that she might have had her vocal cords severed, until one day when I picked her up to take her to the vet for the removal of her last tooth, which was infected. When I arrived at the house, she ran and waited at the door. My mom was on the phone, so Taffy barked to say, "Let her in!"

We were shocked! My mom soon adopted Taffy because she loved having her around.

A few months later my mom called me crying. Taffy was acting strange, sleeping all the time, and not wanting to go for her walks. I took her to the vet, and they thought that maybe it was just her age. Their advice was to keep an eye on her.

At 3 a.m. Taffy had a seizure, and my mom called me because she didn't know how to handle it. Since I had worked with vets and had dealt with a few fosters with seizures, I rushed over. I sat with Taffy all night, and she had several more. My mother couldn't handle seeing her like that, so Taffy came home to stay with me, but we went to visit my mom every day.

Nine months after rescuing this sweet little girl who was all kisses, her seizures became worse and uncontrollable. No amount of medication could stop them, which broke our hearts. One day we were walking down the stairs to get into the car, and Taffy went into a seizure, causing her to fall down the stairs. My oldest son scooped her up and held her as we rushed her to the vet.

It took 10 minutes to get to the vet, but I knew in those 10 minutes that it was time to let her go. I didn't want her to suffer anymore. I held her as it was done, and my mom came to say goodbye. Our vet had her cremated for us, and we placed her in the rose garden in the front yard. This little Miss Taffy touched every one of our hearts, and every time the roses bloom we think of her.

 *Niki Maas*

Now, That's a Dog!

L ucy was born about a decade ago somewhere in central New Jersey. No one seems to really know what happened to her or her siblings. She ended up at a pound and was on "doggie death row" when a private humane group put her into a foster home until they could find her a permanent one. As we all know, it is not easy to find a one- or two-year-old Pit/Lab mix a home.

My husband, John, and I were looking for a dog. We had been married several years earlier and weren't yet ready for a child. A dog was to be the start of our family. John looked at bigger dogs; I actually looked at teacup poodles! We were very far apart in our tastes.

During an Internet search one weekend, I stumbled on the Mutt of the Month. It was Sweetie, a dog in central Jersey. I looked into her eyes and fell in love! I printed her picture in color and brought it out to the living room to show John. I will never forget what he said: "Now, that's a dog!" From that moment on, we were on a mission to adopt her.

Sweetie, now Lucy, was living with three Greyhounds and two cats. She was very quiet but wagged her tail like crazy. Her foster mother said Lucy really liked water and could turn on the kitchen sink. Showing off for us, Lucy jumped so high she was almost *in* the sink.

The adoption process was not easy. We had to provide three references and information on our vet (we had no vet... we didn't have a dog yet!). Still, we got through it. Then we had to pay for Lucy to be spayed and pass a home visit. To make sure we'd be approved, we actually had our neighbor cut a door in his fence to the vacant lot next door, so it looked like we had a really big yard!

Anyway, we finally got Lucy. We only heard her make a noise about twice that first year. She never chewed; she never messed in the house. Dream dog.

About a year after we got Lucy, John and I bought a small resort and moved to Costa Rica. Lucy was great on the plane and great at the resort. She just loves company! She is now totally out of her shell, and boy, did she find her voice. She goes nuts over the monkeys, iguanas, pizotes (badger-like animals), and birds. She still has not learned to stay away from skunks or the giant spraying toads, but hey, we live in the jungle. She firmly believes she is protecting us and takes her job very seriously.

Last year Lucy was certified as a service dog, so she never has to be away from us. She is allowed to sit on the plane with us, stay in hotel rooms with us and even go to restaurants with us. However, she is a bit of a food hound, so we try to keep her out of restaurants.

That is Lucy's story, from doggie death row to a 12-acre estate in Costa Rica. Not bad going! Everyone who meets Lucy loves her and thinks she is a very special dog. She makes amazing eye contact and seems to always know if we are hurt or upset; she tries her best to comfort us.

I will never know if she is our dog or if we are her people, but I don't suppose it matters.

 *Amanda Courter & John Bjorklund*

Visiting With Grace

Three years ago a Smooth Collie-mix arrived at the Washington Animal Rescue League. She came to us in one of our transport vans from a shelter on Maryland's eastern shore. And while this is no exception, as dogs from other shelters come to the League almost daily, this one caught the attention of the League's animal welfare director and the transport manager, who brought her to us and so aptly named her Grace. Grace was gentle and clean— even her toenails had been trimmed. Those of us who are accustomed to greeting these animals as they come in to the League by the hundreds never cease to wonder how such beautiful animals can end up in a shelter.

Grace was paired up with Norm, a now legendary little German Shepherd-mix, who recovered at the League from a horridly imbedded collar, and together they were placed front and center in the first dog den on the left as visitors enter the renovated animal recovery facility. Our animal welfare director immediately perceived that Grace was owner-searching, sadly scrutinizing every shelter visitor. "Why am I here? Where is my family?"

Another staffer at the League came to know Grace as a friend when the animal welfare director brought her upstairs for a little relief from the confusion she was experiencing in the shelter. This staffer had a well-loved 14-year-old German Shepherd-mix with a story of his own: Blackie successfully survived surgery for a brain tumor at age 12, and though welcome to come to work, was not at all interested in spending any time in a shelter, thank you. And this staffer almost felt guilty at how taken we all were with Grace.

Blackie passed away peacefully in the 14th year of his life. Many pet guardians need some time to mourn and reflect on their loss, but not this family. They needed a dog in the house right away! Astonishingly, Grace had been at the League for over a month and had not one adoption application pending. She was probably seven and not very small, but still, her availability was a blessing to this family in severe need of canine companionship.

Grace immediately made herself at home, and she helped her new family with happy recollections of dear old Blackie. She slept at the foot of the bed, made Collie noises ("Timmy fell down the well!"), and patrolled the garden for naughty bunnies. She was soon joined by an even naughtier Dachshund, also a little long in the tooth, as we say, but not so big. Grace adores greeting new people at the League every day, visiting with old friends, and meeting strangers everywhere.

Grace was a good girl, but she was to become an angel. The League's director of animal welfare has several wonderful animals. Among them is Shiner, a magnificent blue merle Smooth Collie with impressive experience as a therapy dog. Grace had an uncommon admiration for Shiner, so Grace's new guardian started thinking, with such apparent, well, gracefulness, couldn't Grace qualify as a therapy dog, too? A little poking around on the Internet brought Grace in touch with Pets on Wheels.

Grace's guardian, who refers to herself as overscheduled, submitted an application around Christmas. She promptly received a package as big as the Dachshund, with information on Pets on Wheels, forms, and questionnaires—paperwork! Nevertheless, eventually the guardian, always cognizant of what a special girl she had, managed to complete and submit that paperwork.

The first Pets on Wheels experience for Grace was to meet her guardian's mentor in a library parking lot. She was hugged and petted and had her feet handled and squeezed by a stranger. Her guardian knew she would breeze through this.

Grace's next challenge was a nursing home, where the residents were dearly in need of visitors. First Grace's guardian visited the home with her mentor and her mentor's dog, who has been doing this sort of thing for eight years. Though the guardian was no stranger to nursing home visits, the mentor's experience and direction was invaluable, as she demonstrated how to carefully balance concern for both the residents and the visiting pet.

Grace visited the nursing home with her guardian and her mentor the following week. Initially Grace's job was to case the joint so as not to be frightened by long linoleum hallways, elevators, or wheelchairs. She was visibly uneasy until she realized that she was there to see people. Her guardian had previously met two individuals who responded to the experienced therapy dog, so they started there.

The darling and genteel lady who is completely bedridden was the first to be introduced to Grace. Grace was initially confused by the hospital bed but soon understood that this person was a new friend. The woman's cheerful, "You have made my day!" and her excitement when the guardian assured her they would return the following week cemented the guardian's commitment to pet therapy with Grace.

The gentleman in the Alzheimer's ward, neat as a pin and with charming "old school" manners, held hands with Grace (she doesn't quit at shake) and kissed her beautiful head. He told her that he loved her, but he really didn't have to. Grace knew.

Grace has received no special training; she is just one remarkable dog with a great deal to give, and not just to her overscheduled guardians. Pets on Wheels operates in many counties in Maryland. Hospitals and schools and nursing homes are desperate for visitors. Who knew that 60% of nursing home residents receive no visitors at all? Cats (who commute) and small dogs are welcome, too.

 *Susan Coe Brown*

Wrong Dog

I vowed to rescue and adopt
the most pitiful dog I could find.
A throw-away dog, unloved and unwanted;
old, sick, abused, or blind.

A box was left on a cold winter's night,
on the steps of a Kentucky pound.
Inside shivered two mangy Bostons;
their owner was never found.

I saw their tale on the Internet;
Their story just made me sick.
Starved, beaten, and covered in mites,
between the two, who could pick?

One was almost solid black,
the other brindle with white.
Skin and bones and almost bare,
a horrific and a sorry sight.

We decided to adopt the black one,
so handsome he'd soon be.
The arrangement with the shelter was
to get him ASAP.

A volunteer met us at PetSmart;
we bought some toys and treats.
We got our new dog a collar,
then waited to finally meet.

The lady arrived with a tiny blue crate
containing a mangy mutt.
"Oh my, it's the wrong dog!" I exclaimed,
"You must have the two mixed up."

She said that the black dog died tragically,
not making it through the night.
So instead we'd be getting the "wrong" dog,
Which turned out to be love at first sight.

He sat there shivering in my arms,
And then he licked my nose.
I wrapped him up in a blanket tight,
his head to the tip of his toes.

We rushed and scrambled to get him home,
and quickly called the vet.
I told her he was barely alive,
but he wasn't quite dead just yet!

The vet started treatment for the mange,
And I bathed him twice a week.
He was so shy and scared, which made me sad:
unsure, cautious, and meek.

Some food and some water,
a nice warm meal.
He looked at us questioning,
Unsure how to feel.

He was hot from fever;
so he slept on the sill.
When I think of his past,
I'm angry, baffled, and ill.

Increasing in strength,
time to walk on a lead.
He bucked and rolled,
But I had treats to feed.

This dog had never seen grass,
or the cold of winter's snow.
He approached both with worried eyes,
and took it very slow.

It was time to give him a name,
So we chose it—Wilbur or Willie.
But he prefers to be called Booger,
a fitting name—he's quite silly.

Now Booger's big and strong,
a handsome Boston Boy.
He loves to give "Booger sugars"
and play with every toy.

His favorite things are to dig big holes,
and roll and romp and play.
He's no longer nervous, shy, or scared,
'cause he knows he's here to stay.

He loves to go for bye-bye rides
and explore new smells on a walk.
He would say, "Thank you for saving me!"
if only dogs could talk.

Now he walks with head held high
and loves to play Booger Ball.
I thought he was the "wrong" dog,
but he's the right one after all!

 *Brandy Hacker*

About Happy Tails Books™

Schnauzer Chihuahua Golden Retriever PUG

DACHSHUND German Shepherd Collie Boxer

Labrador Retriever Husky Beagle ALL AMERICAN

Border Collie Pit Bull Terrier Shih Tzu Miniature Pinscher

Chow Chow Australian Shepherd Rottweiler Greyhound

Boston Terrier Jack Russell Poodle Cocker Spaniel

GREAT DANE Doberman Pinscher Yorkie SHEEPDOG

ST. BERNARD Pointer Blue Heeler

Happy Tails Books™ was created to help support animal rescue efforts by showcasing the love and joy adopted dogs have to offer. With the help of animal rescue groups, stories are submitted by people who have adopted dogs, and then Happy Tails Books™ compiles them into breed-specific books. These books serve not only to entertain but also to educate readers about dog adoption and the characteristics of each specific type of dog. Happy Tails Books™ donates a significant portion of proceeds back to the rescue groups that help gather stories for the books.

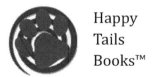

Happy Tails Books™

To submit a story or learn about other books Happy Tails Books™ publishes, please visit our website at http://happytailsbooks.com.